D1319266

A Catalog of Biblical Passages in the Dead Sea Scrolls

Society of Biblical Literature

Text-Critical Studies

Editor
James R. Adair, Jr.

Volume 2
A CATALOG OF BIBLICAL PASSAGES
IN THE DEAD SEA SCROLLS

A CATALOG OF BIBLICAL PASSAGES IN THE DEAD SEA SCROLLS

David L. Washburn

Society of Biblical Literature
Atlanta

A CATALOG OF BIBLICAL PASSAGES
IN THE DEAD SEA SCROLLS

David L. Washburn

Library of Congress Cataloging-in-Publication Data

Washburn, David L.
  A catalog of biblical passages in the Dead Sea scrolls / by David L. Washburn.
    p. cm. — (Text-critical studies ; v. 2)
  Includes bibliographical references.
  ISBN 1-58983-040-7
  1. Bible. O.T.—Quotations—Indexes. 2. Dead Sea scrolls—Quotations. I. Title. II. Series.
BS1099.H4 W37 2002
221.4'4—dc21

                            2002015778

08 07 06 05 04 03 02   5 4 3 2 1

Printed in the United States of America
on acid-free paper

DEDICATION

To Helen Washburn, my late mother,

who always believed in me even when I didn't;

and

to Kathy Washburn, the most precious wife in the universe,

who keeps me believing.

TABLE OF CONTENTS

PREFACE

I produced the original draft of this work in 1983 as a Master's thesis, under the direction of the late Dr. Robert Alden of Denver Seminary. At that time, it provided a complete listing of passages preserved in the published Dead Sea Scrolls. Since then, of course, many more scrolls have been published. This current work should be complete through DJD 35.

Naturally, any such work as this will miss a few items. I hope that discerning readers and reviewers will bear with me and bring omissions that they find to my attention. The publishers and I intend to make this work an ongoing labor, releasing new editions (perhaps in electronic form) as the volume of newly-published material warrants. To make future editions as complete as possible, I ask readers to inform me of passages I have missed (please include bibliographic information!) by contacting me through the publisher or directly.

I would like to thank James Adair for his tireless efforts to get me the materials I needed and to get this work into print.

David L. Washburn
Boise, Idaho
July 2002

INTRODUCTION

Description

The material contained in this volume is intended to be a comprehensive listing of biblical passages contained in all the Dead Sea Scrolls that have been published to date. This list is accompanied by an identification of the scroll containing the passage, publication information on the scroll in question (with references to plates where possible), and a brief description and/or textual analysis.

As used in this book, "Dead Sea Scrolls" refers to the biblical documents (and documents containing biblical citations, such as 1QS) discovered near Khirbet Qumran, Wadi Murabba'at, Naḥal Ḥever, and some other sites. Scholars sometimes include many documents from Egypt's Cairo Genizeh under the heading of Dead Sea Scrolls, but this practice has not been followed here. Only those scrolls and fragments actually associated with the region around the Dead Sea are cited.[1]

Sources

By far the majority of material is published in the series Discoveries in the Judaean Desert (DJD). The volumes of this series that are available contain most of the published scrolls from Qumran and Murabba'at; the major exceptions are 1QIsaᵃ, 1QS, and 1QpHab. (The scrolls of Jeremiah, likewise, were originally published separately and without plates — see the Catalog, though now plates have been published in DJD 15.) For these three major scrolls from Qumran cave 1, the photographic edition by Cross was used.[2] Periodical indexes were also very useful for locating recent finds. It should be noted that the DJD volume containing the Samuel scrolls from Cave 4 was not yet available as of this writing.

---

[1] Elisha Qimron, *The Hebrew of the Dead Sea Scrolls* (Harvard Semitic Studies 29; Atlanta: Scholars Press, 1986) 15, likewise excludes the Cairo documents from his discussion.

[2] Frank M. Cross and others, eds., *Scrolls from Qumran Cave I* (Jerusalem: Albright Institute of Archaeological Research, 1972). This contains photographs of 1QIsaᵃ, 1QS, and 1QpHab.

The Dead Sea Scrolls Phenomenon

The story of the scrolls is well known.[3] Commentators frequently maintain that they prove the reliability of the Masoretic Text (MT) of the Old Testament. Others claim that they prove just the opposite, that the text of the OT was in a great state of flux at the time the scrolls were produced. This catalog will show that both views are oversimplified generalizations. Textual comments compare each fragment with the MT (as represented in *BHS*[4]) and the Septuagint (LXX) text represented in the Rahlfs edition. Other versions, such as the Syriac or the Samaritan Pentateuch, are only noted where a variant of some significance appears and they have bearing on its analysis. Citations of these versions have been taken from *BHS* and from textual notes in the source materials such as the DJD series.

The scrolls, for the most part, do in fact support the MT far more than LXX. To say that this fact indicates the total reliability of the MT as it has come to this century, however, is a gross overstatement. Even the Masoretes recognized certain problems with the text they received, as evidenced by their frequent use of the *Qere* siglum.

Without a doubt, the most striking scroll textually is 8ḤevXII gr, a leather scroll of the Minor Prophets in Greek. This scroll is not an LXX text but is a direct, literal translation of an MT-type text.[5] This may suggest that the authority of LXX in Palestine was not as strong as it was in the diaspora. And in fact, representation of LXX is slim indeed. The only Hebrew scrolls that support it extensively are from cave 4. Scrolls from the other caves (and the rest of those from cave 4) contain LXX variants, but only very sporadically. There are some actual LXX manuscripts from Cave 4, but they are relatively few.

While the caves did contain several Aramaic documents (cave 4 even had some in Latin and Arabic), the only biblical Targums that have been found are fragments of Leviticus and Job from cave 4, and the Targum of Job from cave 11. Why this is so and what it means for the history of language usage in Palestine during the Greek and Roman periods is still a matter of debate, and probably always will be.

The scrolls purported to preserve New Testament passages have been excluded from consideration here, mostly because of the fierce controversy surrounding Father

---

[3] See e.g. F. F. Bruce, *Second Thoughts on the Dead Sea Scrolls* (Grand Rapids: Wm. B. Eerdmans Publishing Co., 1956).

[4] K. Elliger and W., Rudolph, editors, *Biblia hebraica stuttgartensia* (Stuttgart: Deutsche Bibelgesellschaft, 1977).

[5] For discussions of its textual character and its place in the textual history of the Hebrew Bible, see D. Barthélemy, *Les Devanciers d'Aquila: Première publication intégrale du texte des fragments du Dodécapropheton* (*Vetus Testamentum Supplements* 10; Leiden: E. J. Brill, 1963) and Tov's discussion in DJD 8.

O'Callaghan's identification of 7Q5 and its relatives.[6] Inclusion of such materials must be postponed at least until there is more general acceptance of their identification.

Some Scroll Peculiarities

11QPs[a] is an oddity among the DSS. It contains most of the Psalter, but in a very strange order. It includes some apocryphal psalms and makes distinctive interpolations in canonical ones. How it came to be will probably always remain debatable, but its textual usefulness is questionable. My own view is that it was a lectionary of some kind.[7] In the Catalog, the Roman numerals after the 11QPs[a] siglum refer to the columns of the scroll. Thus, for example, 11QPs[a] xvi is column 16.

A few scrolls are in the ancient Hebrew script. Several other scrolls use the ancient script for the Divine Name, and some extend this practice to the name *El* as well. These phenomena seem to indicate that some of the scribes may have attached some special significance to the old script and held it in some sort of reverence or considered its use more respectful when referring to God or the holy books. This attitude of preferring older forms of language when dealing with God is strikingly like the attitude of some Christians today, who feel that the antiquated English pronouns "thee" and "thou" are somehow more reverent when addressing God (note this practice in the NASB and RSV).

In the Qumran script especially, and to a lesser degree in the scrolls of the other locations, the letters *waw* and *yodh* are often written identically. This sometimes causes confusion when reading a passage, but the places where this is a real problem are relatively few.[8] Sometimes this problem of identification also occurs with *he* and *ḥeth*. The ancient scribes wrote *he* with a small tittle, thus: ꧑, while they made *ḥeth* without it: ꧑. If the tittle is small, or the top stroke of the *ḥeth* is carelessly made, confusion may arise, and sometimes does.

Final forms of letters are fairly infrequent. This is especially true of *kaph*, partly because second person pronominal suffixes were often written fully, כה, rather than defectively, ך, as in later manuscripts. But in many instances of other letters with final forms, the normal form occurs where a final form would appear in the medieval manuscripts. In the passages that are written out in the catalog, I have tried to reproduce final forms as they actually occur in the scrolls.

---

[6] In light of recent work such as Robert H. Gundry, "No *NU* in Line 2 of 7Q5: A Final Disidentification of 7Q5 with Mark 6:52-53," *JBL* 118 (1999):698-707, acceptance of these scrolls as fragments of the New Testament is not likely to happen.

[7] Cf. P. W. Flint, *The Dead Sea Psalms Scroll and the Book of Psalms,* STDJ 17 (Leiden: Brill, 1997).

[8] Cf. Russell Fuller, "Text-Critical Problems in Malachi 2:10-16," *JBL* 110 (1991): 47-57, for some examples of places where this phenomenon produces difficulties. A scroll that distinguishes the letters fairly well is 4QDeut[h]. See J. A. Duncan, "New Readings for the 'Blessing of Moses' from Qumran," *JBL* 114 (1995): 273-290.

Confusion of person and number in verbs and suffixes is common in the scrolls. This probably points not to differing textual traditions, but to confusion of similar letters and a touch of human error. Comparatively few of these variants are attested by other manuscripts or versions.

Format

This volume is designed to be a reference work for scholars, commentators, teachers, and students who wish to investigate Dead Sea Scroll representation of any given biblical passage or book. Apocryphal/Deuterocanonical books are not included. Citations follow the order of the Christian (Protestant) canon.

Where two or more passages in the scrolls overlap, the sequence in the catalog follows the first verse of any given portion. For example, 4Qphyl[h] contains Deuteronomy 5:22-6:5, while 1Qphyl preserves Deuteronomy 5:23-27. Although the former extends far beyond the latter, 4Qphyl[h] begins a verse before 1Qphyl and is therefore listed before 1Qphyl in the catalog.

In the case of two or more citations beginning at the same verse, the shortest citation is listed first. Deuteronomy 5 provides a good example of this, as well. Seven documents begin with Deuteronomy 5:1. 4Qphyl[a] extends to 5:14, while the others extend to 5:16, 21, 22, 24; 6:1, and 6:5. They are listed in this order. This has the effect of somewhat preserving the sequence of the chapter, continuously extending beyond the previous point. Most of this sequential arrangement occurs in the Torah, but some was also necessary in Psalms, Isaiah, and the Minor Prophets.

No real textual analysis of 1QIsa[a] is given here. Studies of the Great Isaiah Scroll are many and varied, and its true textual character is still a matter of some debate. It seemed best to refer the reader to these studies[9], or, better yet, to the manuscript itself. The photographic edition[10] is well referenced, and location of a given passage in it is not difficult. Since the textual affinities of an ancient manuscript will vary from one passage to another, it seems far more sensible to evaluate each passage or variant on its own merits than to try to assign the entire scroll to a particular text-type or simply to pronounce it a "mixed text."

Many of the more fragmentary passages are written out fully. The chief criterion used for deciding what to write out and what not to is length. Some readings that are unique to the scrolls are written out as well, if the reading seems interesting enough to warrant comment and/or further study.

---

[9] For a comprehensive listing, see J. A. Fitzmyer, *The Dead Sea Scrolls: Major Publications and Tools for Study*, rev. ed, SBL Resources for Biblical Study 20 (Atlanta: Scholars Press, 1990).

[10] See note 2 above.

Terms Used in the Catalog

Identical to ...

Indicates that the scroll described agrees with . . (usually MT) in text, spelling and word order.

Follows ...

Indicates that text and word order are the same as . . . but spelling may vary, especially with regard to *plene* forms.

Mostly follows ...

Variations in text are confined to word order, inclusion/exclusion of the article or conjunction, and similar minor matters.

Mostly follows ... except ...

Any major variants are noted as indicated.

Generally follows ...

Some variation from the text indicated, but variants are unique to the DSS themselves and are not supported by LXX or other versions, except where specifically noted.

Corresponds to ...

In the Targum of Job, this indicates a reasonably literal translation of the text noted.

Fragmentary

Only portions of the passage remain, frequently as few as two or three letters of any verse. Some of these are noted specifically. Where a verse within a given passage is not represented, this has been indicated in the passage listing rather than in the textual notes.

JBL	*Journal of Biblical Literature*
Jub	The Book of Jubilees
LXX	Septuagint
M	Milḥamah (the War Scroll)
Mas	Masada
Melch	Melchizedek
mez	Mezuza, portion of the Torah bound on a door post
MT	Masoretic text
Mur	Wadi Murabba'at
N/R	Not represented
OTS	*Oudtestamentische Studiën*
paleo	The text is written in Paleo-Hebrew script
paraph	Paraphrase
p, Pesher	Running commentary on the biblical text, noted by "p" in the scroll sigla
phyl	Phylactery
Q	Qumran; in the scroll sigla, the number preceding indicates in which Qumran cave the particular manuscript was found
RB	*Revue biblique*
RevQ	*Revue de Qumran*
S	Serek Hay-yaḥad (that is, the Manual of Discipline)

Sam	Samaritan Pentateuch
Syr	Syriac version
SWDS	Frank Moore Cross, *Scrolls from the Wilderness of the Dead Sea*
t, tg	Targum, used in the scroll sigla
Testim	Testimonia
v., vv.	verse(s)
vis	vision, used in the siglum of one of the Samuel scrolls from cave 4
VT	*Vetus Testamentum*
VTSup	Vetus Testamentum Supplements
XII	Twelve Minor Prophets
ZAW	*Zeitschrift für die alttestamentliche Wissenschaft*
(?)	Identification uncertain
[ ]	Indicates that letters within the bracket(s) have been reconstructed and are not on the fragment
;	Separates comments in the notes. What follows the semicolon is not related to what precedes
,	Separates comments in the notes. What follows is a continuation of what precedes
בּ	A dot under a letter indicates that the letter's identification is uncertain

THE CATALOG

Reference	Scroll	Location	Comments
Gen 1:1-11	4QGen^g (4Q7)	DJD 12:58	Fragmentary; mostly follows MT.
Gen 1:1-25	4QGen^b (4Q2)	DJD 12:33-34	Follows MT.
Gen 1:8-10	4QGen^{h1} (4Q8)	DJD 12:61	Very fragmentary; follows MT.
Gen 1:9	4QGen^k (4Q10)	DJD 12:76	וַתֵּרָא הִיבָ Of no textual value.
Gen 1:13-22	4QGen^g (4Q7)	DJD12:59-60	Fragmentary; mostly follows MT.
Gen 1:14-16	4QGen^k (4Q10)	DJD 12:77	Fragmentary; mostly follows MT.
Gen 1:18-21 (v. 19 N/R)	1QGen (1Q1)	DJD 1:49	אל]הים כי יש]רוצו המים שר א]ל]הים ישרצו v. 20. MT
Gen 1:18-27	4QGen^d (4Q4)	DJD 12:44	Fragmentary; follows MT.
Gen 1:27-28	4QGen^k (4Q10)	DJD 12:77	Very fragmentary; identical to MT.

Reference	Scroll	Location	Comments
Gen 1:28-29(?)	4Q483	Puech, *Revue De Qumran* 74 (1999): 259-260.	Baillet in DJD 7 questions this identification, suggesting it could be either Gen or Jubilees. Of no textual value.
Gen 2:1-3	4QGen^k (4Q10)	DJD 12:78	Very fragmentary; identical to MT.
Gen 2:6-7 or 18-19	4QGen^g (4Q7)	DJD 12:60	Of no textual value.
Gen 2:14-19	4QGen^b (4Q2)	DJD 12:36	Fragmentary; follows MT.
Gen 2:17-18	4QGen^{h2} (4Q8)	DJD 12:62	Very fragmentary; identical to MT.
Gen 2:24	4QInstruction^b (4Q416)	DJD 34:123	Very fragmentary; identical to MT.
Gen 3:1-2	4QGen^k (4Q10)	DJD 12:78	Very fragmentary; supports *BHS* emendation האף in v. 1.
Gen 3:11-14	1QGen (1Q1)	DJD 1:49	Fragmentary; v. 11 appears to read ער[ום] for MT עירם.
Gen 4:2-11	4QGen^b (4Q2)	DJD 12:36-37	Identical to MT.
Gen 5:13 or 14	4QGen^b (4Q2)	DJD 12:37	קינן Of no textual value.
Gen 6:13-21	6QpaleoGen (6Q1)	DJD 3:105	Archaic script; fragmentary; follows MT
Gen 6:15	4QCommentary on Gen D (4Q254a)	DJD 22:234	Of no textual value.
Gen 7:11	4QCommentary on Gen A (4Q252)	DJD 22:193	Commentary material splits the verse in 2; mostly follows MT.
Gen 8:5a	4QCommentary on Gen A (4Q252)	DJD 22:194	Follows MT.

Reference	Scroll	Location	Comments
Gen 8:13	4QCommentary on Gen A (4Q252)	DJD 22:194	Follows MT.
Gen 8:20-21(?)	4QGen-Exod[a] (4Q1)	DJD 12:29-30	Of no textual value.
Gen 9:24	4QCommentary on Gen A (4Q252)	DJD 22:198	Follows MT.
Gen 9:24-25	4QCommentary on Gen C (4Q254)	DJD 22:220	Fragmentary; follows MT.
Gen 9:25	4QCommentary on Gen A (4Q252)	DJD 22:198	Follows MT with some spelling variations.
Gen 12:4-5	4QGen[h-para] (4Q8)	DJD 12:62	Of no textual value.
Gen 12:18-15:4	1QApGen	Fitzmyer, *Gen Apocryphon*	Fairly complete with many interpolations. In Aramaic; fairly literal where it follows Gen.
Gen 17:12-19	8Q1	DJD 3:147	Extremely fragmentary; of no textual value.
Gen 18:20-25	8Q1	DJD 3:147-148	Extremely fragmentary; identical to MT except interlinear note [א[תהדבר over כדבר in v. 25.
Gen 19:27-28	2Q1	DJD 3:48	[ש[ם את פני [ס[דם ועמרה Identical to MT.
Gen 21:9-10	4Q365	DJD 13:263	Follows MT.
Gen 22:10	4QCommentary on Gen A (4Q252)	DJD 22:201	Follows MT.

Reference	*Scroll*	*Location*	*Comments*
Gen 22:13-15	1QGen (1Q1)	DJD 1:49	Fragmentary; follows MT.
Gen 22:14	4QGen-Exodᵃ (4Q1)	*JBL* 110:577-582	Small fragment; reads אלהים for יהוה
Gen 23:17-19	1QGen (1Q1)	DJD 1:49	Fragmentary; identical to MT.
Gen 24:22-24	1QGen (1Q1)	DJD 1:50	הנגמ[לל]י[ם ידי[ה עשרה ותא[מ]ר אל[יו Identical to MT.
Gen 25:9, 7-8 (?)	2QJubᵃ (2Q19)	DJD 3:78	Paraphrase with additions; of no textual value for Gen.
Gen 25:18-21	4Q364	DJD 13:205	Semi-paraphrase.
Gen 26:7-8	4Q364	DJD 13:205	Fragmentary; follows MT with 1 unique reading.
Gen 26:21-28 (2 letters v. 28)	4QpaleoGenesisᵐ (4Q12)	DJD 9:51	Fragmentary; follows MT.
Gen 27:38-39	4QGen-Exodᵃ (4Q1)	DJD 12:11	Extremely fragmentary; identical to MT.
Gen 27:42-43	4QGen-Exodᵃ (4Q1)	DJD 12:11	Extremely fragmentary; identical to MT.
Gen 28:6	4Q364	DJD 13:207	Pesher precedes; follows MT.
Gen 29:32-33(?)	4Q364	DJD 13:207	Identification questionable.
Gen 30:8-14 (v. 10 N/R; 2 letters each vv. 8 & 9)	4Q364	DJD 13:208	Follows MT with unique expansion.
Gen 30:26-36 (v. 34 N/R)	4Q364	DJD 13:209-210	Mostly follows MT; adds a paraphrase of Gen 31:11-13 after v. 36.

Reference	Scroll	Location	Comments
Gen 31:47-53	4Q364	DJD 13:211	Fragmentary; generally follows MT.
Gen 32:4-5	MurGen (Mur1)	DJD 2:75	Fragmentary; identical to MT.
Gen 32:18-20	4Q364	DJD 13:212	Follows MT.
Gen 32:25-32	4Q158	DJD 5:1	Follows MT.
Gen 32:26-30 (1 word v. 26)	4Q364	DJD 13:213	Generally follows LXX.
Gen 32:30, 33 to 33:1	MurGen (Mur1)	DJD 2:76	Fragmentary; identical to MT.
Gen 34:2(?)	4Q364	DJD 13:214	נְשִׂיא הָאָרֶץ תְ
Gen 34:5-7	MurGen (Mur1)	DJD 2:76	Very fragmentary; identical to MT.
Gen 34:7-10 (v. 8 N/R)	4Q576	DJD 25:193	Very fragmentary; follows MT.
Gen 34:17 21	4QGen-Exodᵃ (4Q1)	DJD 12:11	Very fragmentary; identical to MT.
Gen 34:30-35:1, 4-7	MurGen (Mur1)	DJD 2:76-77	Extremely fragmentary; identical to MT.
Gen 35:6-10 (v. 9 N/R)	HevGen	Burchard, *ZAW* 78:73	Very fragmentary; follows MT.
Gen 35:17-36:13 (36:1,11 N/R)	4QGen-Exodᵃ (4Q1)	DJD 12:12	Fragmentary; follows MT; supports *Qere* reading in 36:5.
Gen 35:28	4Q364	DJD 13:214	מִי יִשְׂחָק מֵאָת שָׁנָה
Gen 36:5-12	HevGen	Burchard, *ZAW* 78:73	Fragmentary; follows MT.
Gen 36:6 (?)	2Q1	DJD 3:48	אֶת מִקְנֵהֶן בְּאָרֶץ Of no textual value.

Reference	*Scroll*	*Location*	*Comments*
Gen 36:12	4QCommentary on Gen A (4Q252)	DJD 22:203	Follows MT except לו for לאליפז.
Gen 36:19-27 (vv. 20, 23 N/R)	4QGen-Exodᵃ (4Q1)	DJD 12:14	Follows MT.
Gen 36:35-37	2Q1	DJD 3:48-49	עַ שמלה ממש שֹׁא Identical to MT.
Gen 36:43-37:2	4QGenᵉ (4Q5)	DJD 12:48	Fragmentary; identical to MT.
Gen 37:5-6	4QGen-Exodᵃ (4Q1)	DJD 12:14	Very fragmentary; identical to MT.
Gen 37:7-8 (1 letter v. 8)	4Q364	DJD 13:215	Follows MT.
Gen 37:22-27	4QGen-Exodᵃ (4Q1)	DJD 12:14-15	Very fragmentary; identical to MT.
Gen 37:27-30	4QGenᵉ (4Q5)	DJD 12:48	Fragmentary; identical to MT.
Gen 38:14-21 (v. 15 N/R; 1 letter v.17)	4Q364	DJD 13:215-216	Follows MT.
Gen 39:11-40:1	4QGen-Exodᵃ (4Q1)	DJD 12:15	Supports *Kethib* in 39:20; follows MT.
Gen 40:12-13	4QGenᶜ (4Q3)	DJD 12:40	זה אֹ פרעה
Gen 40:18?/19?-41:8	4QGenᵉ (4Q5)	DJD 12:49	Generally follows MT with some unique readings; tends to read רקות (=Sam) for MT דקות.
Gen 40:18-41:11 (40:21-22 N/R)	4QGenᶜ (4Q3)	DJD 12:40-41	Generally follows MT with some peculiarities.

Reference	Scroll	Location	Comments
Gen 41:35-44	4QGenᵉ (4Q5)	DJD 12:50	Follows MT except reads תכרד for MT תכרת v. 36.
Gen 41:15-18	4QGenʲ (4Q9)	DJD 12:66	Adds לא above the line in v. 16 before יענה (=LXX, Sam).
Gen 41:23-27	4QGenʲ (4Q9)	DJD 12:67	Follows MT except adds שבע above the line in v. 24.
Gen 41:29-36	4QGenʲ (4Q9)	DJD 12:68	Follows MT except ויקמו for MT וקמו v. 30.
Gen 41:38-43	4QGenʲ (4Q9)	DJD 12:69	Follows MT with one unique reading? DJD reads ממוך for MT כמוך in line 3. Upon examining the plate, I confess I don't see anything but a lacuna where the editors read ממ. It is, however, a somewhat poor photo.
Gen 42:15-22	4QGenʲ (4Q9)	DJD 12:69	Mostly follows MT.
Gen 42:17-19	4QGenᵉ (4Q5)	DJD 12:51	Very fragmentary, follows MT.
Gen 42:38-43:2	4QGenʲ (4Q9)	DJD 12:70	Fragmentary; identical to MT.
Gen 43:5-8	4QGenʲ (4Q9)	DJD 12:70	Fragmentary; identical to MT.
Gen 43:8-14	4QGenᵉ (4Q5)	DJD 12:51	Follows MT with spelling variations.
Gen 44:30-45:1	4Q364	DJD 13:216-217	Follows MT with pesher insertion before 45:1.
Gen 45:14-22	4QGenʲ (4Q9)	DJD 12:71	Fragmentary; follows MT with some spelling errors.
Gen 45:21-27	4Q364	DJD 13:218	Generally follows MT.
Gen 45:23	4QGen-Exodᵃ (4Q1)	DJD 12:16	וְת נשָׂא Of no textual value.

Reference	Scroll	Location	Comments
Gen 45:26-28	4QGenʲ (4Q9)	DJD 12:72	Very fragmentary; identical to MT.
Gen 47:13-14 (1 letter of v. 13)	4QGen-Exodᵃ (4Q1)	DJD 12:16	Of no textual value.
Gen 48:1-11	4QGenᶠ (4Q6)	DJD 12:54	Omits ואקברה שם בדרך אפרת אל אביו v. 7; omits v. 9; changes word order v. 10; otherwise follows MT.
Gen 48:2-4	4QGen-Exodᵃ (4Q1)	DJD 12:17	Of no textual value.
Gen 48:14-15(?)	4Q364	DJD 13:219	Fragmentary; follows MT.
Gen 48:15-17	4QGen-Exodᵃ (4Q1)	DJD 12:17	Fragmentary; identical to MT.
Gen 48:18-22	4QGen-Exodᵃ (4Q1)	DJD 12:17	Fragmentary; identical to MT.
Gen 49:1-5	4QGen-Exodᵃ (4Q1)	DJD 12:17-18	Very fragmentary; identical to MT.
Gen 49:3a	4QCommentary on Gen A (4Q252)	DJD 22:203	Omits פחי (=LXXᵐˢˢ).
Gen 49:4a	4QCommentary on Gen A (4Q252)	DJD 22:203	Reads פחזתה (=LXX); omits כי (unique).
Gen 49:6-8	4QGenᵉ (4Q5)	DJD 12:52	Very fragmentary; follows MT.
Gen 49:15-17	4QCommentary on Gen C (4Q254)	DJD 22:224	Very fragmentary; generally follows MT.
Gen 49:24-26 (2 letters v. 26)	4QCommentary on Gen C (4Q254)	DJD 22:225	Only sure variant follows Sam.
Gen 50:3	4Q576	DJD 25:193	חנטי Of no textual value.

Reference	Scroll	Location	Comments
Gen 50:26?	4QpaleoGen-Exod[l] (4Q11)	DJD 9:25	בְמ
Gen 50:26, 22 (?)	2QJub[b] (2Q20)	DJD 3:79	Paraphrase; of no textual value.

Reference	Scroll	Location	Comments
Exod 1:1-5 (v. 3 N/R)	4QpaleoGen-Exod[l] (4Q11)	DJD 9:25	Mostly follows MT.
Exod 1:1-5?	4QpaleoGen-Exod[l] (4Q11)	DJD 9:47	Of no textual value.
Exod 1:1-6	4QExod[b] (4Q13)	DJD 12:84	Fragmentary; generally follows LXX.
Exod 1:3-17	4QGen-Exod[a] (4Q1)	DJD 12:18	Follows MT except reads שבעים] וחמש v. 5 (LXX= אחמש שבעים
Exod 1:7	2Q20	DJD 3:79	Extremely fragmentary; of no textual value.
Exod 1:11-14	2QExod[a] (2Q2)	DJD 3:49	Fragmentary; mostly follows MT.
Exod 1:16-21	4QExod[b] (4Q13)	DJD 12:86	Generally follows MT with some minor variation.
Exod 1:22-2:5	4QGen-Exod[a] (4Q1)	DJD 12.19	Mostly follows MT.
Exod 2:2-18	4QExod[b] (4Q13)	DJD 12:87	Strange addition v. 3; otherwise generally follows LXX.
Exod 2:10	4QpaleoGen-Exod[l] (4Q11)	DJD 9:26	שׁ[מ][ן משה
Exod 2:22-3:4	4QpaleoGen-Exod[l] (4Q11)	DJD 9:27	Follows MT except ויצעקן for ויזעקן (=MT[mss], Sam).

Reference	Scroll	Location	Comments
Exod 3:8-16 (1 letter v. 16)	4QGen-Exod^a (4Q1)	DJD 12:20	Follows MT with some unique readings.
Exod 3:12	4Q158	DJD 5:2	העם ממצרים תעבד[ון Identical to MT.
Exod 3:13-21	4QExod^b (4Q13)	DJD 12:90	A puzzling array of variants, many unique.
Exod 3:17-21	4QpaleoGen-Exod^l (4Q11)	DJD 9:28	Very fragmentary; identical to MT.
Exod 3:18-21	4QGen-Exod^a (4Q1)	DJD 12:22	Very fragmentary; follows MT.
Exod 4:1-8	4QExod^b (4Q13)	DJD 12:91	Fragmentary; all non-MT readings are unique; otherwise follows MT.
Exod 4:4-9	4QGen-Exod^a (4Q1)	DJD 12:22	Very fragmentary; follows MT.
Exod 4:26-5:1	4QGen-Exod^a (4Q1)	DJD 12:23	Fragmentary; identical to MT.
Exod 4:27-28	4Q158	DJD 5:1	Loose paraphrase; of no textual value.
Exod 4:28-31	MurExod (Mur1)	DJD 2:77	Identical to MT.
Exod 4:31	2Q3	DJD 3:53	וישמע[ו] ויקד[ו] Of no textual value.
Exod 5:3	MurExod (Mur1)	DJD 2:77	Extremely fragmentary; of no textual value.
Exod 5:3,5	2QExod^c (2Q4) (2Q4)	DJD 3:56	Of no textual value.
Exod 5:3-14	4QExod^b (4Q13)	DJD 12:93-94	Fragmentary; most non-MT readings follow LXX or are unique.

Reference	Scroll	Location	Comments
Exod 5:3-17	4QGen-Exodᵃ (4Q1)	DJD 12:24-25	Follows MT.
Exod 6:3-6	4QExodʰ (4Q19)	DJD 12:147	Fragmentary; follows MT.
Exod 6:4-21 (1 word v. 4)	4QGen-Exodᵃ (4Q1)	DJD 12:25-26	Fragmentary; follows MT with 1 unique reading.
Exod 6:5-11	Mur Exod (Mur1)	DJD 2:77-78	Identical to MT.
Exod 6:25	4QGen-Exodᵃ (4Q1)	DJD 12:26	Of no textual value.
Exod 6:25-7:16 (1 word 7:16)	4QpaleoExodᵐ (4Q22)	DJD 9:72-73	Generally follows MT.
Exod 6:25-7:19	4QpaleoExodᵐ (4Q22)	*SWDS* 14, 24	Archaic script; similar to Sam.
Exod 7:1-4	2Q2	DJD 3:50	Fragmentary; identical to MT.
Exod 7:5-13	4QGen-Exodᵃ (4Q1)	DJD 12:27	Follows MT with 1 LXX reading (לפני for אל v. 10).
Exod 7:15-20 (1 word v. 20)	4QGen-Exodᵃ (4Q1)	DJD 12:28	Mostly follows MT.
Exod 7:16-19	4QpaleoExodᵐ (4Q22)	DJD 9:74-75	Includes addition to v. 8 from Sam (but addition has several unique readings); otherwise follows MT.
Exod 7:17-23 (v.18 N/R)	4QExodᶜ (4Q14)	DJD 12:103	Very fragmentary; follows MT with several unusual spellings.
Exod 7:26-8:1 (7:29 N/R)	4QExodᶜ (4Q14)	DJD 12:104	Very fragmentary; follows MT.
Exod 7:29b-8:1 (1 word 8:1)	4QpaleoExodᵐ (4Q22)	DJD 9:76	7:29b is an addition from Sam; fragmentary.
Exod 7:29b -8:1b (7:28-8:2?)	4QExodʲ (4Q20)	DJD 12:150	Extremely fragmentary; of no textual value.

Reference	*Scroll*	*Location*	*Comments*
Exod 8:5-14 (v.10 N/R)	4QExodᶜ (4Q14)	DJD 12:104	Fragmentary; mostly follows MT.
Exod 8:12-18 (1 letter v. 18)	4QpaleoExodᵐ (4Q22)	DJD 9:76	Very fragmentary; follows MT with a couple of unique readings.
Exod 8:13-15 (1 letter v. 13)	4QpaleoGen-Exodˡ (4Q11)	DJD 9:28	Extremely fragmentary; of no textual value.
Exod 8:13-19	4Q365	DJD 13:263	Generally follows MT.
Exod 8:16-18	4QExodᶜ (4Q14)	DJD 12:104	Fragmentary; mostly follows MT.
Exod 8:19-21 (1 letter v. 21)	4QpaleoGen-Exodˡ (4Q11)	DJD 9:29	Very fragmentary; identical to MT.
Exod 8:19b-22 (1 partial word v. 22)	4QpaleoExodᵐ (4Q22)	DJD 9:77	8:19b is an addition from Sam; otherwise follows MT.
Exod 8:20-22	4QGen-Exodᵃ (4Q1)	DJD 12:28	Of no textual value.
Exod 8:22	4QExodᶜ (4Q14)	DJD 12:106	Of no textual value.
Exod 9:5b-16 (1 letter v. 15; 1 partial word v. 16)	4QpaleoExodᵐ (4Q22)	DJD 9:78-79	9:5b is an addition from Sam; generally follows Sam.
Exod 9:8(?)	4QGen-Exodᵃ (4Q1)	DJD 12:28	מֹר יְ שַׁ מֹימֹה
Exod 9:9-12	4Q365	DJD 13:265	Follows MT.
Exod 9:11	4QExodᶜ (4Q14)	DJD 12:107	טמים ובכל מ
Exod 9:15-20 (v. 17 N/R)	4QExodᶜ (4Q14)	DJD 12:107	Fragmentary; follows MT.
Exod 9:19b-21 (3 letters v. 21)	4QpaleoExodᵐ (4Q22)	DJD 9:79	9:19b is an addition from Sam; very fragmentary; otherwise follows MT.
Exod 9:22-25	4QExodᶜ (4Q14)	DJD 12:107	Fragmentary; follows MT.

Reference	*Scroll*	*Location*	*Comments*
Exod 9:25-29 (1 letter v. 26)	4QpaleoGen-Exod¹ (4Q11)	DJD 9:29	Fragmentary; follows MT.
Exod 9:27-29	2Q2	DJD 3:50	Fragmentary; follows MT.
Exod 9:27-35	4QExodᶜ (4Q14)	DJD 12:107	Fragmentary; generally follows MT.
Exod 9:33-10:5 (2 letters 10:5)	4QpaleoGen-Exod¹ (4Q11)	DJD 9:30	Follows MT except את before עמי 10:3.
Exod 9:35-10:1	4QpaleoExodᵐ (4Q22)	DJD 9:81	Extremely fragmentary; follows MT.
Exod 10:1-5	4QExodᶜ (4Q14)	DJD 12:110	Very fragmentary; follows MT.
Exod 10:2b-5	4QpaleoExodᵐ (4Q22)	DJD 9:81	10:2b is an addition from Sam; otherwise of no textual value.
Exod 10:5-12	4QpaleoExodᵐ (4Q22)	DJD 9:82	Includes Sam addition v. 5; otherwise follows MT.
Exod 10:7-9	4QExodᶜ (4Q14)	DJD 12:110	Very fragmentary; follows MT.
Exod 10:12-19	4QExodᶜ (4Q14)	DJD 12:110	Very fragmentary; non-MT readings follow LXX.
Exod 10:19?-20	4Q365	DJD 13:265	Of no textual value.
Exod 10:19-24 (3 letters v. 20)	4QpaleoExodᵐ (4Q22)	DJD 9:82	Fragmentary; sometimes follows Sam, sometimes MT.
Exod 10:23-24	4QExodᶜ (4Q14)	DJD 12:111	Extremely fragmentary; identical to MT.
Exod 10:25-28	4QpaleoExodᵐ (4Q22)	DJD 9:84	נשאר v. 26 (=LXX); otherwise follows MT.
Exod 11:4-12:12	4QpaleoGen-Exod¹ (4Q11)	DJD 9:31-32	Fragmentary; generally follows MT.
Exod 11:3-7	2Q2	DJD 3:50	Fragmentary; mostly follows MT.

Reference	Scroll	Location	Comments
Exod 11:8-12:2	4QpaleoExod^m (4Q22)	DJD 9:84	Omits וֹ of וַיֹּאמֶר 11:9. DJD does not note this reading but it is clear on the plate.
Exod 11:9-10	4QExod^c (4Q14)	DJD 12:113	Very fragmentary; identical to MT.
Exod 12:6-8 (2 letters v. 8)	4QpaleoExod^m (4Q22)	DJD 9:85	Very fragmentary; generally follows MT.
Exod 12:12-16	4QExod^c (4Q14)	DJD 12:113	Fragmentary; follows MT.
Exod 12:13-15	4QpaleoExod^m (4Q22)	DJD 9:85	Fragmentary; follows MT.
Exod 12:17-22 (2 letters v. 17; 1 letter v. 22)	4QpaleoExod^m (4Q22)	DJD 9:86	Very fragmentary; follows MT.
Exod 12:26-27 (?)	2Q3	DJD 3:53	סֶמֶ א֞ אֲשֶׁר פֶּ ת מִצְרַיִם Of no textual value.
Exod 12:31-32 (2 letters v. 32)	4QpaleoExod^m (4Q22)	DJD 9:87	Extremely fragmentary; follows MT.
Exod 12:31-48	4QExod^c (4Q14)	DJD 12:114	Generally follows MT with several scribal errors.
Exod 12:32-41	2Q2	DJD 3:51	Fragmentary; follows MT.
Exod 12:34-39	4QpaleoExod^m (4Q22)	DJD 9:87	Follows MT with several spelling variations.
Exod 12:42-46 (v. 45 N/R)	4QpaleoGen-Exod^l (4Q11)	DJD 9:33	Fragmentary; follows MT.
Exod 12:43-44	4QDeut^j (4Q37)	DJD 14:88	Of no textual value.
Exod 12:43-13:7	4Qphyl^a (4Q128)	DJD 6:50-51	Extremely fragmentary; favors LXX.
Exod 12:43-13:10 (many vv. N/R)	4Qphylⁱ (4Q136)	DJD 6:63	Fragmentary; follows MT.

Reference	Scroll	Location	Comments
Exod 12:44-13:10 (many vv. N/R)	4Qphyl^m (4Q140)	DJD 6:71-72	Very fragmentary; a wide array of MT, LXX, Sam, and unique readings.
Exod 12:46-13:5 (12:47 N/R)	4QDeut^j (4Q37)	DJD 14:89	Very fragmentary; follows MT with a couple of unique readings.
Exod 13:1-4 (2 letters of v. 4)	4Qmez^f (4Q154)	DJD 6:84	Fragmentary; follows MT.
Exod 13:1-10 (vv. 3, 4, 10 N/R)	4Qphyl^e (4Q132)	DJD 6:57	Of no textual value.
Exod 13:1-10	4Qphyl^r (4Q145)	DJD 6:77-78	Fragmentary; mostly follows MT.
Exod 13:1-16	Murphyl (Mur4)	DJD 2:81-83	Text complete; identical to MT, including paragraph divisions.
Exod 13:1-16 (v. 2 N/R)	4Qphyl^c (4Q130)	DJD 6:54	Somewhat fragmentary; mostly follows MT.
Exod 13:2-3	1Qphyl (1Q13)	DJD 1:75	Fragmentary; identical to MT.
Exod 13:3-5	4QExod^c (4Q16)	DJD 12:130	A very inconsistent array of variants.
Exod 13:3-7	4QpaleoExod^m (4Q22)	DJD 9:88	Very fragmentary; follows MT.
Exod 13:4-9 (more vv. absent than present)	4Qphyl^u (4Q144)	DJD 6:76	Fragmentary; no certain variants.
Exod 13:7-9	1Qphyl (1Q13)	DJD 1:75	Very fragmentary; identical to MT.
Exod 13:9-16	4Qphyl^b (4Q129)	DJD 6:53	Fragmentary; mostly follows Sam.
Exod 13:11-16	4Qphyl^f (4Q133)	DJD 6:57	Extremely fragmentary; follows MT.
Exod 13:11-16	4Qmez^g (155)	DJD 6:84-85	Follows MT.

Reference	*Scroll*	*Location*	*Comments*
Exod 13:12-13	4QpaleoExod^m (4Q22)	DJD 9:88	גֵּר בפרה בשה
Exod 13:14-16	4Qphyl^h (4Q135)	DJD 6:62	Generally follows MT with some Sam readings.
Exod 13:15-16	4QExod^d (4Q15)	DJD 12:128	Fragmentary; follows MT.
Exod 13:18-14:13 (14:1, 6 N/R)	4QExod^c (4Q14)	DJD 12:114-117	Very fragmentary; mostly follows MT.
Exod 14:3-5	4QpaleoExod^m (4Q22)	DJD 9:89	Very fragmentary; follows MT.
Exod 14:8-9	4QpaleoExod^m (4Q22)	DJD 9:89	Very fragmentary; follows MT.
Exod 14:10	4Q365	DJD 13:266	Generally follows Sam with some unique additions.
Exod 14:12-21	4Q365	DJD 13:266-267	Unique addition v. 17; duplicates part of v. 20 in v. 19.
Exod 14:15-24	4QpaleoGen-Exod^l (4Q11)	DJD 9:34	Fragmentary; follows MT.
Exod 14:21-27	4QExod^g (4Q18)	DJD 12:145	Very fragmentary; identical to MT.
Exod 14:25	4QpaleoExod^m (4Q22)	DJD 9:90	Of no textual value; DJD lists as vv. 25-26, but no text from v. 26 remains.
Exod 15:1	4QExod^d (4Q15)	DJD 12:128	Fragmentary; identical to MT.
Exod 15:9-21 (v. 10 N/R)	4QExod^c (4Q14)	DJD 12:117-118	Generally follows MT with some Sam and some unique readings.
Exod 15:16-20	4Q365	DJD 13:268	Mostly follows MT; unique addition v. 19.
Exod 15:17-18	4QFlor (4Q174)	DJD 5:53	Six words; follows MT.

Reference	*Scroll*	*Location*	*Comments*
Exod 15:23-16:1	4QpaleoExod^m (4Q22)	DJD 9:90-91	Fragmentary; follows MT.
Exod 16:2-6	4QpaleoGen-Exod^l (4Q11)	DJD 9:35	Fragmentary; follows MT.
Exod 16:4-5	4QpaleoExod^m (4Q22)	DJD 9:91	Of no textual value.
Exod 16:7	4QpaleoGen-Exod^l (4Q11)	DJD 9:36	עָ תלִינֻוּ follows MT *Qere*.
Exod 16:7-8 (4 letters v. 8)	4QpaleoExod^m (4Q22)	DJD 9:91	Of no textual value.
Exod 16:12-16	1QExod (1Q2)	DJD 1:50	Fragmentary; v. 14 has כְהסֹפֹס for MT מֹחסֹפֹס (=LXX ωσει).
Exod 16:13-14 (1 letter v. 14)	4QpaleoGen-Exod^l (4Q11)	DJD 9:36	Of no textual value.
Exod 16:23-25	4QpaleoGen-Exod^l (4Q11)	DJD 9:37	Very fragmentary; identical to MT.
Exod 16:26-31	4QpaleoGen-Exod^l (4Q11)	DJD 9:37	Very fragmentary; follows MT.
Exod 16:31-32	4QpaleoExod^m (4Q22)	DJD 9:92	Very fragmentary; follows MT.
Exod 16:32-17:16	4QpaleoExod^m (4Q22)	DJD 9:92-93	Fragmentary; text is predominantly Sam.
Exod 16:33-17:3 (16:36 N/R)	4QpaleoGen-Exod^l (4Q11)	DJD 9:38	Fragmentary; generally follows MT.
Exod 17:1-18:12	4QExod^c (4Q14)	DJD 12:120-121	Fragmentary; generally follows MT with some minor variants.
Exod 17:3-5	4Q365	DJD 13:272	Several unique readings; reads 1st person plural pronouns v. 3 (=LXX)

Reference	Scroll	Location	Comments
Exod 17:5-11 (2 letters v. 8)	4QpaleoGen-Exodˡ (4Q11)	DJD 9:39	Very fragmentary; follows MT.
Exod 17:16-18:21 (18:19 N/R)	4QpaleoExodᵐ (4Q22)	DJD 9:95	Very fragmentary; most variants are unique.
Exod 18:13-16	4Q365	DJD 13:273	Fragmentary; conflates LXX (יתר) and MT (חותן מושה) v. 14.
Exod 18:17-24	4QpaleoGen-Exodˡ (4Q11)	DJD 9:40	Generally follows MT.
Exod 18:21-22	2QExodᵇ (2Q3) (2Q3)	DJD 3:53	וָא ‏אנשי אמ ‏רי מאיות ‏כול Of no textual value
Exod 18:21-19:1 (3 letters 19:1)	4QpaleoExodᵐ (4Q22)	DJD 9:97	Includes Sam addition at 18:25; otherwise generally follows MT.
Exod 19:7-17	4QpaleoExodᵐ (4Q22)	DJD 9:99-100	Very fragmentary; follows MT.
Exod 19:9	2QExodᵇ (2Q3) (2Q3)	DJD 3:55	ם ריגד מושה Of no textual value.
Exod 19:17(?)	4Q364	DJD 13:221	בתחתית ההר
Exod 19:17-23 (vv. 18,20 N/R)	4Q158	DJD 5:3	Of no textual value.
Exod 19:23-20:1	4QpaleoExodᵐ (4Q22)	DJD 9:100	Fragmentary; follows MT.
Exod 19:24-20:1	1QExod (1Q2)	DJD 1:51	Fragmentary; identical to MT.
Exod 19:24-20:2	4QpaleoGen-Exodˡ (4Q11)	DJD 9:41	Very fragmentary; identical to MT.
Exod 20:5-6 (?)	1QExod (1Q2)	DJD 1:51	Fragmentary; of no textual value.

Reference	Scroll	Location	Comments
Exod 20:7-12	4Qmezᵃ (149)	DJD 6:80-81	Fragmentary; textual value questionable.
Exod 20:12, 16, 17	4Q158	DJD 5:3	Extremely fragmentary; identical to MT.
Exod 20:18-19a (1 word v. 18)	4QpaleoExodᵐ (4Q22)	DJD 9:101	20:19a is a Sam addition.
Exod 20:19-22	4Q158	DJD 5:3	Fragmentary; follows MT.
Exod 20:21	4Q175	DJD 5:57	Similar to Sam.
Exod 20:22-21:1, 3, 4, 6, 10	4Q158	DJD 5:3-4	Very fragmentary; follows MT.
Exod 20:25-21:1, 4-5	1QExod (1Q2)	DJD 1:51	Extremely fragmentary; of no textual value.
Exod 21:5-6	4QpaleoExodᵐ (4Q22)	DJD 9:103	Follows MT.
Exod 21:13-14	4QpaleoExodᵐ (4Q22)	DJD 9:104	Very fragmentary; mostly follows MT.
Exod 21:14-22 (1 word v. 15; v. 16-18 N/R)	4Q364	DJD 13:220	Follows MT except יקם for ויקם v. 21.
Exod 21:15,16, 18, 20, 22, 25	4Q158	DJD 5:4	Extremely fragmentary; of no textual value.
Exod 21:22-32 (v. 23 N/R)	4QpaleoExodᵐ (4Q22)	DJD 9:104	Very fragmentary; follows MT.
Exod 21:28-29	4Q251	DJD 35:33	Paraphrase of no textual value; note that DJD erroneously lists it as a paraphrase of Exod 21:26-27.
Exod 21:32, 34, 35 to 22:13	4Q158	DJD 5:5	Very fragmentary; assorted departures from MT in all directions.

Reference	*Scroll*	*Location*	*Comments*
Exod 21:35-22:5	4Q366	DJD 13:337	Fragmentary; may support some Sam/LXX additions to 22:4.
Exod 21:37-22:2 (?)	2QExod^b (2Q3)	DJD 3:53	אִישׁ שׁ תחת הש מָלָא ה מֹשׁ עָ לם Of no textual value.
Exod 22:3-4	4QpaleoExod^m (4Q22)	DJD 9:105	Very fragmentary; follows Sam.
Exod 22:6-7	4QpaleoExod^m (4Q22)	DJD 9:105	Very fragmentary; only variant follows Sam.
Exod 22:11-13 (1 letter v. 11)	4QpaleoExod^m (4Q22)	DJD 9:106	Extremely fragmentary; identical to MT.
Exod 22:15-19	2QExod^b (2Q3) (2Q3)	DJD 3:54	Of no textual value.
Exod 22:16-19 (v. 17 N/R; 1 letter v. 19)	4QpaleoExod^m (4Q22)	DJD 9:106	Of no textual value.
Exod 22:20-30 (v. 21 N/R; 1 letter v. 20)	4QpaleoExod^m (4Q22)	DJD 9:106-107	Fragmentary; follows MT.
Exod 22:23-24	4QpaleoGen-Exod^l (4Q11)	DJD 9:41	Extremely fragmentary; identical to MT.
Exod 23:5-16 (v. 14 N/R)	4QpaleoGen-Exod^l (4Q11)	DJD 9:42	Variants lean toward versions and other MSS of MT.
Exod 23:7a	1QS 5:15	Cross, *Scrolls from Qumran Cave 1*	Only non-MT reading follows LXX.
Exod 24:12	4QJubilees^a (4Q216)	DJD 13:5	הָאֶבֶן הַתוֹר[ה] (MT= והתורה)

Reference	Scroll	Location	Comments
Exod 24:12-14	4Q364	DJD 13:221	Generally follows MT with some unique readings.
Exod 23:15-16	4QpaleoExod^m (4Q22)	DJD 9:107	Of no textual value.
Exod 23:29-31 (3 letters v. 30)	4QpaleoExod^m (4Q22)	DJD 9:108	Very fragmentary; only suggested variant is questionable.
Exod 24:1-4	4QpaleoExod^m (4Q22)	DJD 9:108	Very fragmentary; follows Sam.
Exod 24:6-11	4QpaleoExod^m (4Q22)	DJD 9:108	Very fragmentary; follows Sam.
Exod 24:18-25:2	4Q364	DJD 13:222	Follows MT with commentary before 25:1.
Exod 25:7-20 (v. 8, 10 N/R; 2 letters v. 16; v. 17 N/R)	4QpaleoGen-Exod^l (4Q11)	DJD 9:43	Very fragmentary; may omit סביב v. 11.
Exod 25:11-12	4QpaleoExod^m (4Q22)	DJD 9:109	Very fragmentary; follows MT.
Exod 25:20-22	4QpaleoExod^m (4Q22)	DJD 9:109	Identification questionable; follows Sam if correct.
Exod 25:22-29	4QpaleoExod^m (4Q22)	DJD 9:110	Fragmentary; mostly follows MT.
Exod 25:31-34	4QpaleoExod^m (4Q22)	DJD 9:110	Very fragmentary; follows MT.
Exod 26:1	4Q364	DJD 13:223	שכן חע בים מ Of no textual value.
Exod 26:8-15	4QpaleoExod^m (4Q22)	DJD 9:111	Fragmentary; mostly follows MT.

Reference	Scroll	Location	Comments
Exod 30:10	4QpaleoExod^m (4Q22)	DJD 9:112	Fragmentary; follows MT.
Exod 30:12-18 (3 letters v. 12; 3 letters v. 14; 1 complete letter v. 17)	4QpaleoExod^m (4Q22)	DJD 9:119	Very fragmentary; column may omit 30:1-10 (=Sam).
Exod 30:23-25	2QExod^a (2Q2)	DJD 3:52	Fragmentary; follows MT.
Exod 30:29-31	4QpaleoExod^m (4Q22)	DJD 9:120	Of no textual value.
Exod 30:32,34	4Q158	DJD 5:6	Fragmentary; mostly follows MT.
Exod 30:34-31:7	4QpaleoExod^m (4Q22)	DJD 9:120-121	Fragmentary; follows MT with a couple of scribal errors.
Exod 30:37-31:2 (31:1 N/R)	4Q365	DJD 13:276	Unique textual character.
Exod 31:7-8	4QpaleoExod^m (4Q22)	DJD 9:122	כל כל ואת
Exod 31:13-15	4QpaleoExod^m (4Q22)	DJD 9:122	Accidentally omits part of vv. 13-14; otherwise follows MT.
Exod 31:16-17 (?)	2QExod^b (2Q3)	DJD 3:54	בת לל⸱א י ישר
Exod 32:2-9 (3 letters v. 5)	4QpaleoExod^m (4Q22)	DJD 9:122-123	Fragmentary; generally follows MT except לא[מ]ור v. 7 (=LXX) and omits לך v. 7 (unique).
Exod 32:10-19 (2 letters v. 19)	4QpaleoExod^m (4Q22)	DJD 9:124	Generally follows Sam including addition in v. 10.
Exod 32:25-30 (2 letters v. 25)	4QpaleoExod^m (4Q22)	DJD 9:124-125	Fragmentary; mostly follows Sam.
Exod 32:32-24 (?)	2QExod^a (2Q2)	DJD 3:52	Of no textual value.

Reference	Scroll	Location	Comments
Exod 33:12-15 (v. 14 N/R)	4QpaleoExod^m (4Q22)	DJD 9:126	Very fragmentary; follows MT.
Exod 33:16-34:3	4QpaleoExod^m (4Q22)	DJD 9:126-127	Very fragmentary; generally follows MT.
Exod 34:10	2QExod^b (2Q3)	DJD 3:55	Fragmentary; may add [משה אל] א[ל[ז] with MT manuscripts after ויאמר.
Exod 34:10-13	4QpaleoExod^m (4Q22)	DJD 9:127	Very fragmentary; generally follows Sam with some scribal errors.
Exod 34:15-18	4QpaleoExod^m (4Q22)	DJD 9:128	Fragmentary; suggested variants seem to be scribal errors.
Exod 34:20-24	4QpaleoExod^m (4Q22)	DJD 9:128	Very fragmentary; follows MT.
Exod 34:27	4Q271	DJD 18:178	Replaces both instances of את with עם; otherwise follows MT.
Exod 34:27-28	4QpaleoExod^m (4Q22)	DJD 9:128	כי על ויהי ם
Exod 35:1	4QpaleoExod^m (4Q22)	DJD 9:129	Of no textual value.
Exod 35:3-5	4Q365	DJD 13.277	Fragmentary; follows MT.
Exod 36:9-10	4QExod^k (4Q21)	DJD 12:151	Fragmentary; identical to MT.
Exod 36:21-24 (3 letters v. 21)	4QpaleoExod^m (4Q22)	DJD 9:129	Fragmentary; follows MT.
Exod 36:32-38	4Q365	DJD 13:278	Fragmentary; non-MT readings are unique or follow LXX.
Exod 36:34-36	4QpaleoGen-Exod^l (4Q11)	DJD 9:47	Very fragmentary; identical to MT.

Reference	*Scroll*	*Location*	*Comments*
Exod 37:9-16	4QpaleoExod^m (4Q22)	DJD 9:130	Fragmentary; על for ל v. 13 (=Syr); otherwise follows MT.
Exod 37:29-38:7	4Q365	DJD 13:279	Unique textual character; most verbs are plural where all other witnesses are singular.
Exod 38:18-22	4QExod-Lev^f (4Q17)	DJD 12:137	No more than 4 letters of any verse; of no textual value.
Exod 39:1-16	4Q365	DJD 13:280-281	Deliberately omits vv. 6-7; numerous other unique oddities.
Exod 39:3-19 (1 letter v. 3; v. 4 N/R?)	4QExod-Lev^f (4Q17)	DJD 12:137-138	Extremely fragmentary; textual value questionable.
Exod 39:17-19	4Q365	DJD 13:283	Fragmentary; follows MT.
Exod 39:20-24	4QExod-Lev^f (4Q17)	DJD 12:139	Fragmentary; generally follows MT.
Exod 40:8-27	4QExod-Lev^f (4Q17)	DJD 12:140-141	Follows MT except for numerous unique scribal errors.
Exod 40:15?	4QpaleoGen-Exod^l (4Q11)	DJD 9:48	Of no textual value.
Lev 1:1-7 (No certain letters v. 7)	4QLev^c (4Q25)	DJD 12:189-190	Very fragmentary; identical to MT.
Lev 1:11	4QpapLXX Lev^b (4Q120)	DJD 9:169	Extremely fragmentary; of no textual value.
Lev 1:11-3:1	4QLev^b (4Q24)	DJD 12:179	Fragmentary; generally follows MT with a couple of LXX readings and several unique readings.

Reference	*Scroll*	*Location*	*Comments*
Lev 1:13-15	4QExod-Lev^f (4Q17)	DJD 12:143	9 letters total; of no textual value.
Lev 1:17-2:1	4QExod-Lev^f (4Q17)	DJD 12:143	Extremely fragmentary; 1 LXX reading and 1 unique.
Lev 2:3-5	4QpapLXX Lev^b (4Q120)	DJD 9:169	Extremely fragmentary; mostly follows LXX/MT.
Lev 2:7-8?	4QpapLXX Lev^b (4Q120)	DJD 9:169	Of no textual value.
Lev 3:4	4QpapLXX Lev^b (4Q120)	DJD 9:170	Fragmentary; απο for LXX/MT επι (unique).
Lev 3:7	4QpapLXX Lev^b (4Q120)	DJD 9:170	ρνα ρο
Lev 3:2-8	4QLev^e (4Q26a)	DJD 12:197-198	Very fragmentary; follows MT.
Lev 3.8-14	4QLev^b (4Q24)	DJD 12:180	Very fragmentary; mostly follows MT.
Lev 3:9-13	4QpapLXX Lev^b (4Q120)	DJD 9:170-171	Fragmentary; mostly follows LXX.
Lev 3:13-14 (4 letters each verse)	4QpapLXX Lev^b (4Q120)	DJD 9:171	Only suggested variant is in a lacuna; of no textual value.
Lev 3:16-4:1 (1 letter 3:16; 1 letter 4.1)	4QIsa^c (4Q57) (see DJD note)	DJD 15:74	Of no textual value.
Lev 3:16-4:6	4QLev^c (4Q25)	DJD 12:190	Fragmentary; identical to MT.
Lev 4:3-4	4QpapLXX Lev^b (4Q120)	DJD 9:171	Extremely fragmentary; εισαχ[ει] for LXX προσαχει
Lev 4:3-9	MasLev^a	Yadin, *IEJ* 15:104 (no plate)	"Agrees with MT both in contents and spelling" [Yadin in *IEJ*].

Reference	*Scroll*	*Location*	*Comments*
Lev 4:4	4QpapLXX Lev[b] (4Q120)	DJD 9:172	Extremely fragmentary; follows LXX.
Lev 4:6-8	4QpapLXX Lev[b] (4Q120)	DJD 9:172	Very fragmentary; follows LXX except της [καρ]π[ωσ]εως for των ολοκαυτωματων (=several minuscules LXX) v. 7.
Lev 4:10-11	4QpapLXX Lev[b] (4Q120)	DJD 9:173	Very fragmentary; follows LXX.
Lev 4:12-14	4QLev[c] (4Q25)	DJD 12:191	Fragmentary; mostly follows MT.
Lev 4:18-19	4QpapLXX Lev[b] (4Q120)	DJD 9:173	Very fragmentary; only listed variant is uncertain.
Lev 4:23-28 (1 letter v. 27)	4QLev[c] (4Q25)	DJD 12:191	Very fragmentary; follows MT.
Lev 4:24-26	11QpaleoLev (11Q1)	Freedman, *11QpaleoLev (11Q1)* 26.	Passage identification uncertain.
Lev 4:26	4QpapLXX Lev[b] (4Q120)	DJD 9:174	Very fragmentary; identical to LXX.
Lev 4:26-28 (1 word v. 26)	4QpapLXX Lev[b] (4Q120)	DJD 9:174	Fragmentary; some unique readings.
Lev 4:30	4QpapLXX Lev[b] (4Q120)	DJD 9:175	τωι δ α κερα υτω
Lev 5:6	4QpapLXX Lev[b] (4Q120)	DJD 9:175	της αμα σεται
Lev 5:8-10	4QpapLXX Lev[b] (4Q120)	DJD 9:175	Fragmentary; mostly follows LXX.
Lev 5:12-13	4QLev[c] (4Q25)	DJD 12:192	Extremely fragmentary; follows MT.

Reference	Scroll	Location	Comments
Lev 5:16-17 (5 letters v. 16; 4 letters v. 17)	4QpapLXX Lev^b (4Q120)	DJD 9:176	Of no textual value.
Lev 5:18-6:5 (MT 5:18-24; 4 letters 6:1; 2 letters 6:5)	4QpapLXX Lev^b (4Q120)	DJD 9:176	Very fragmentary; some unique readings; εις τ[ον Ιαω] 6:2/5:21 (=MT).
Lev 7:19-26 (v. 22 N/R)	4QLev^g (4Q26b)	DJD 12:203	Fragmentary; mostly follows MT; interesting use of archaic *lamed* v. 25.
Lev 7:34-35	11QLev^b (11Q2)	DJD 23:3	בְּנֵי אֵשׁ
Lev 8:12-13	6QpaleoLev (6Q2)	DJD 3:106	Archaic script; fragmentary; identical to MT.
Lev 8:26-28	4QLev^c (4Q25)	DJD 12:192	Very fragmentary; identical to MT.
Lev 8:31-34 (v. 32 N/R; 1 letter v. 33, 34)	MasLev^b	Talmon, *Eretz Israel* 106	Of no textual value.
Lev 9:1-10 (1 letter v. 7)	MasLev^b	Talmon, *Eretz Israel* 106	Fragmentary; identical to MT.
Lev 9:12-13	MasLev^b	Talmon, *Eretz Israel* 107	Of no textual value.
Lev 9:22-24	MasLev^b	Talmon, *Eretz Israel* 107	Very fragmentary; identical to MT.
Lev 9:23-10:2	11QLev^b (11Q2)	DJD 23:3-4	Fragmentary; generally follows LXX.
Lev 10:4-7	11QpaleoLev (11Q1)	Freedman, *11QpaleoLev (11Q1)* 27.	Fragmentary; mostly follows MT.
Lev 10:9-20	MasLev^b	Talmon, *Eretz Israel* 108	Very fragmentary; identical to MT.

Reference	*Scroll*	*Location*	*Comments*
Lev 11:1-2	4Q365	DJD 13:284	דְבַר יה חָיה אֹתָ
Lev 11:1-21 (1 letter v. 1; 1 letter v. 14; 3 letters v. 19; 3 letters v. 20)	MasLev[b]	Talmon, *Eretz Israel* 109	Very fragmentary; extant text identical to MT; see article for speculation about variants in lacunae.
Lev 11:10-11	1QLev (1Q3)	DJD 1:52	Archaic script; fragmentary; identical to MT.
Lev 11:17-24 (v. 18, 19 N/R)	4Q365	DJD 13:284	Very fragmentary; generally follows MT.
Lev 11:22-29	2QPaleoLev (2Q5)	DJD 3:56	Fragmentary; archaic script; follows MT.
Lev 11:24-40 (1 letter v. 25)	MasLev[b]	Talmon, *Eretz Israel* 110	Identical to MT.
Lev 11:27-32	11QpaleoLev (11Q1)	Freedman, *11QpaleoLev (11Q1)* 28.	נח]ון for כפיו v. 27; otherwise follows MT.
Lev 11:32	4Q365	DJD 13:285	Generally follows MT.
Lev 11:40-45 (v. 43 N/R)	4Q365	DJD 13:286	Fragmentary; most significant readings listed are reconstructions.
Lev 11:47-13:1	4Q367	DJD 13:347	Fragmentary; mostly follows MT.
Lev 12:1-4	4Q265	DJD 35:70	Loose paraphrase of no textual value. Note divergences in restoration between DJD and García Martínez, *Study Edition*.
Lev 13 and 15	4QD[a] (4Q266)	Milik, *RB* 73:105	Halakah on these chapters; of no textual value.

Reference	Scroll	Location	Comments
Lev 13:3-9	11QpaleoLev (11Q1)	Freedman, *11QpaleoLev (11Q1)* 29.	Fragmentary; follows MT.
Lev 13:6-8 (1 letter v. 8)	4Q365	DJD 13:287	Very fragmentary; follows MT.
Lev 13:15-18 (v. 16 N/R)	4Q365	DJD 13:288	Extremely fragmentary; follows MT?
Lev 13:32-33	4QLev-Num^a (4Q23)	DJD 12:156	Of no textual value.
Lev 13:33	4Q272	DJD 18:188	Very fragmentary; follows MT.
Lev 13:39-43 (v. 41 N/R)	11QpaleoLev (11Q1)	Freedman, *11QpaleoLev (11Q1)* 30.	Very fragmentary; קרחת v. 42 (=LXX);otherwise follows MT.
Lev 13:51-52	4Q365	DJD 13:288	Extremely fragmentary; follows MT.
Lev 13:45-46	4Q274	DJD 35.100	Fragmentary; of no textual value.
Lev 13:58-59	11QLev^b (11Q2)	DJD 23:5	Fragmentary; mostly follows MT with several unique readings.
Lev 14:8	4Q396	DJD 10:54	Paraphrase of no textual value.
Lev 14:16-17 (1 letter v. 17)	11QLev^b (11Q2)	DJD 23:6	צבעו ש פ
Lev 14:16-21	11QpaleoLev (11Q1)	Freedman, *11QpaleoLev (11Q1)* 31.	Omits אצבעו v. 16 (=Sam); several scribal errors.
Lev 14:22-34	4QLev-Num^a (4Q23)	DJD 12:156	Fragmentary; follows MT.
Lev 14:27-29	4QLev^d (4Q26)	DJD 12:193	Very fragmentary; follows MT.
Lev 14:33-36	4QLev^d (4Q26)	DJD 12:194	Very fragmentary; follows MT with 1 unique reading.

Reference	*Scroll*	*Location*	*Comments*
Lev 14:40-54	4QLev-Num[a] (4Q23)	DJD 12:157-158	Fragmentary; follows MT with several unique readings.
Lev 14:52-15:5 (14:56 & 15:1 N/R; 1 letter each 14:52, 55)	11QpaleoLev (11Q1)	Freedman, *11QpaleoLev (11Q1)* 32.	LXX addition in 15:3; otherwise follows MT.
Lev 15:3; 17:2-4; 18:27 to 19:3; 20:2-3; 21:6-9; 22:22-25; 24:9-10; 25:29-35; 26:20-24; 27:13-17	11QpaleoLev (11Q1)	Freedman, *CBQ* 36: 525-534 (no plate)	Gives only variants from MT. Apparently quite fragmentary. Arrangement of article is awkward.
Lev 15:10-11	4QLev-Num[a] (4Q23)	DJD 12:158	Very fragmentary; identical to MT.
Lev 15:14-15	4Q367	DJD 13:348	Follows MT.
Lev 15:18-19 (2 letters v. 18)	11QLev[b] (11Q2)	DJD 23:6	Extremely fragmentary; follows MT.
Lev 15:19-24	4QLev-Num[a] (4Q23)	DJD 12:159	Very fragmentary; identical to MT.
Lev 15:20-24 (1 letter v. 23)	4QLev[d] (4Q26)	DJD 12:194	Very fragmentary; follows MT.
Lev 16:2-4	11QpaleoLev (11Q1)	Freedman, *11QpaleoLev (11Q1)* 32.	Of no textual value.
Lev 16:11-12(?)	4Q365	DJD 13:289	Editors also suggest vv. 6-7 or 17-18; of no textual value.
Lev 16:12-21 (v. 16-17 N/R)	4QtLev (4Q156)	DJD 6:87	Fragmentary; in Aramaic; corresponds to MT.
Lev 16:15-29	4QLev-Num[a] (4Q23)	DJD 12:159	Fragmentary; mostly follows MT.

Reference	Scroll	Location	Comments
Lev 16:34-17:5	11QpaleoLev (11Q1)	Freedman, *11QpaleoLev (11Q1)* 34.	A couple of scribal errors; otherwise follows MT.
Lev 17:2-11	4QLev^d (4Q26)	DJD 12:194-195	Fragmentary; generally follows LXX.
Lev 17:3	4Q394	DJD 10:48	Reads ו for MT אֹו.
Lev 18:16-21 (v. 19 N/R; 1 letter v. 20)	4QLev-Num^a (4Q23)	DJD 12:160	Fragmentary; identical to MT.
Lev 18:26-28	4Q365	DJD 13:290	Extremely fragmentary; follows MT.
Lev 18:27-19:4	11QpaleoLev (11Q1)	Freedman, *11QpaleoLev (11Q1)* 36.	Accidentally adds and then deletes part of 20:4 in 18:27; generally follows MT.
Lev 19:1-4	4Q367	DJD 13:348	Follows MT.
Lev 19:3-8	4QLev-Num^a (4Q23)	DJD 12:160	Fragmentary; follows MT.
Lev 19:6	4Q394	DJD 10:46 (Note misprint that lists this verse as 19.16)	Paraphrase of no textual value.
Lev 19:9-15	4Q367	DJD 13:348-349	Follows MT.
Lev 19:17	4Q270	DJD 18:159	כָ ח ת
Lev 19:30-34	1QLev (1Q3)	DJD 1:52	Archaic script; fragmentary; identical to MT.
Lev 19:34-37	4QLev^e (4Q26a)	DJD 12:198	Fragmentary; generally follows MT.
Lev 20:1-3 (1 letter v. 1)	4QLev^e (4Q26a)	DJD 12:198	Extremely fragmentary; identical to MT.

Reference	*Scroll*	*Location*	*Comments*
Lev 20:1-6	11QpaleoLev (11Q1)	Freedman, *11QpaleoLev (11Q1)* 38.	Generally follows MT.
Lev 20:13	4Q367	DJD 13:350	Fragmentary; follows MT.
Lev 20:20-24	1QLev (1Q3)	DJD 1:52	Archaic script; fragmentary; mostly follows MT.
Lev 20:27-21:4	4QLevᵉ (4Q26a)	DJD 12:199	Fragmentary; mostly follows MT.
Lev 21:6-11	11QpaleoLev (11Q1)	Freedman, *11QpaleoLev (11Q1)* 39.	Some affinities with Sam.
Lev 21:9-12	4QLevᵉ (4Q26a)	DJD 12:199	Fragmentary; generally follows MT.
Lev 21:17-20 (v. 19 N/R)	4QLevᵇ (4Q24)	DJD 12:181	1 word of each verse; of no textual value.
Lev 21:21-24	4QLevᵉ (4Q26a)	DJD 12:200	Omits בני v. 24; otherwise follows MT.
Lev 21:24-22:6 (22:1 N/R)	1QLev (1Q3)	DJD 1:52-53	Archaic script; fragmentary; follows MT.
Lev 21:24-23:1	4QLevᵇ (4Q24)	DJD 12:181-182	Fragmentary; most readings are unique.
Lev 22:4-6	4QLevᵉ (4Q26a)	DJD 12:200	Extremely fragmentary; only non-MT reading follows LXX.
Lev 22:21-27 (v. 26 N/R)	11QpaleoLev (11Q1)	Freedman, *11QpaleoLev (11Q1)* 41.	Follows MT with some scribal errors.
Lev 22:11-17	4QLevᵉ (4Q26a)	DJD 12:201	Fragmentary; identical to MT.
Lev 23:2-25	4QLevᵇ (4Q24)	DJD 12:183-184	Mostly follows MT.
Lev 23:4-8	1QLev (1Q3)	DJD 1:53	Archaic script; fragmentary; identical to MT.

Reference	Scroll	Location	Comments
Lev 23:22-29	11QpaleoLev (11Q1)	Freedman, *11QpaleoLev (11Q1)* 42.	Follows MT.
Lev 23:28	4Q271	DJD 18:180	Omits יהוה; otherwise follows MT.
Lev 23:38	4Q270	DJD 18:161	Omits יהוה.
Lev 23:40	4QLev^b (4Q24)	DJD 12:185	Of no textual value.
Lev 23:42-24:2a	4Q365	DJD 13:290-291	Generally follows MT; 24:2a serves as an intro to some extrabiblical material.
Lev 24:2-23	4QLev^b (4Q24)	DJD 12:185-186	Mostly follows MT.
Lev 24:9-14	11QpaleoLev (11Q1)	Freedman, *11QpaleoLev (11Q1)* 43.	ויניחו אתו for MT ויניחהו; otherwise follows MT.
Lev 24:11-12	4QLev-Num^a (4Q23)	DJD 12:161	Of no textual value.
Lev 24:20-22(?) (2 letters v. 20; v. 21 N/R)	4Q366	DJD 13:339	Identification uncertain; Lev 25:39-43 follows.
Lev 25:7-9	4Q365	DJD 13:296	Fragmentary; textual character fluctuates.
Lev 25:9	11QMelch (11Q13) 26	van der Woude, *OTS* 14:358	והעברתמהשופן]בָחֹן[ ]הָ Of no textual value.
Lev 25:10 (?)	11QMelch (11Q13) 6	van der Woude, *OTS* 14:358	וקרא להמה דרר MT reads וקראתם דרור
Lev 25:13	11QMelch (11Q13) 2	van der Woude, *OTS* 14:358	בשנת היו] [Identical to MT.
Lev 25:14	4Q271	DJD 18:175	לוא for MT אל; עמיתו for MT אחיו; otherwise follows MT.

Reference	*Scroll*	*Location*	*Comments*
Lev 25:28-29	4QLev[b] (4Q24)	DJD 12:186	Fragmentary; identical to MT.
Lev 25:28-36	11QpaleoLev (11Q1)	Freedman, *11QpaleoLev (11Q1)* 44.	Follows MT with many scribal errors.
Lev 25:31-33	11QLev[b] (11Q2)	DJD 23:7	Very fragmentary; mostly follows MT; note ביתו ע]יר v. 33 (MT= בית ועיר).
Lev 25:39-43 (1 letter v. 43)	4Q366	DJD 13:339	Generally follows MT with 1 unique addition v. 41.
Lev 25:45-52 (v. 50 N/R)	4QLev[b] (4Q24)	DJD 12:186	Follows MT except 1 LXX reading v. 46.
Lev 26:2-16	4QLXX Lev[a] (4Q119)	DJD 9:162 see also *SWDS* 13, 23	Fragmentary; many deviations from LXX toward versional and unique readings.
Lev 26:17-26	11QpaleoLev (11Q1)	Freedman, *11QpaleoLev (11Q1)* 46.	Mostly follows MT; most non-MT readings are scribal errors.
Lev 26:17-32 (v. 29 N/R)	4Q365	DJD 13:296-297	Some MT, some LXX, some Sam and some unique readings.
Lev 26:26-33	4QLev-Num[a] (4Q23)	DJD 12:161	Fragmentary; follows MT.
Lev 26:44	4Q463	DJD 19:211	Omits זאת; reads ארצות (=Sam); may have a unique addition after בריתי, but it is difficult to tell where quote ends.
Lev 27:5-22	4QLev-Num[a] (4Q23)	DJD 12:161-162	Fragmentary; mostly follows MT.
Lev 27:11-19	11QpaleoLev (11Q1)	Freedman, *11QpaleoLev (11Q1)* 48.	Mostly follows MT; several scribal errors and variant spellings.

Reference	Scroll	Location	Comments
Lev 27:30-31 (?)	1QLev (1Q3)	DJD 1:54	Identification uncertain; only six letters total.
Lev 27:30-34	4Q367	DJD 13:350	Follows MT.
Lev 27:34(?)	4Q365	DJD 13:299	Identification questionable.

Reference	Scroll	Location	Comments
Num 1:1-5 (1 letter v. 5)	4Q365	DJD 13:299	Generally follows MT.
Num 1:1-5 (3 letters each vv. 4 & 5)	4QLev-Numᵃ (4Q23)	DJD 12:163	Fragmentary; identical to MT.
Num 1:21-22	4QLev-Numᵃ (4Q23)	DJD 12:163	Fragmentary; identical to MT.
Num 1:36-40 (1 letter v. 37)	4QLev-Numᵃ (4Q23)	DJD 12:163	Fragmentary; follows MT.
Num 1:48-50	1QLev (1Q3)	DJD 1:53	Archaic script; יֹ תפקד וֹ ךֹ אֶתֹ identical to MT
Num 2:18-20 (v. 19 N/R; 1 letter v. 20)	4QLev-Numᵃ (4Q23)	DJD 12:164	Of no textual value.
Num 2:31-32	4QLev-Numᵃ (4Q23)	DJD 12:164	Fragmentary; identical to MT.
Num 3:3-19 (v. 17 N/R; 1 letter v. 19)	4QLev-Numᵃ (4Q23)	DJD 12:164	Generally follows MT.
Num 3:26-30	4Q365	DJD 13:300	Most non-MT readings are unique.
Num 3:38-41	2QNumᵃ (2Q6)	DJD 3:57	Fragmentary; follows MT.

Reference	Scroll	Location	Comments
Num 3:40-42	4QLXXNum (4Q121)	Skehan, VTSup 4:155-156	Fragmentary; text uncertain.
Num 3:40-43	4QLXXNum (4Q121)	DJD 9:189	Very fragmentary; a couple of unique readings; πρωτο]τοκο[ν α]ρσεν v. 43 (=MT).
Num 3:50-51?	4QLXXNum (4Q121)	DJD 9:190	Identification very questionable.
Num 3:51-4:3	2QNumᵃ (2Q6)	DJD 3:58	Extremely fragmentary; follows MT.
Num 3:51-4:12	4QLev-Numᵃ (4Q23)	DJD 12:165	Identical to MT.
Num 4:1?	4QLXXNum (4Q121)	DJD 9:191	Of no textual value.
Num 4:5-9	4QLXXNum (4Q121)	DJD 9:191	Fragmentary; non-unique readings favor MT.
Num 4:6-9	4QLXXNum (4Q121)	Skehan, *BA* 28:91-92	Fragmentary; wavers between LXX and MT.
Num 4:11-16	4QLXXNum (4Q121)	DJD 9:192-193	Fragmentary; most non-MT readings are unique.
Num 4:40-5:9	4QLev-Numᵃ (4Q23)	DJD 12:166-167	Fragmentary; mostly follows MT.
Num 4:47-49	4Q365	DJD 13:301	Mostly follows MT.
Num 7:1	4Q365	DJD 13:301	Follows MT.
Num 7:78-80 (4 letters v. 80)	4Q365	DJD 13:302	Mostly follows MT.
Num 7:88	2QNumᶜ (2Q8)	DJD 3:59	אָרְב [ ] פרים[שנה ששים Identical to MT.
Num 8:7-12	4QLev-Numᵃ (4Q23)	DJD 12:167	Fragmentary; identical to MT.

Reference	Scroll	Location	Comments
Num 8:11-12	4Q365	DJD 13:303	Of no textual value.
Num 8:21-22	4QLev-Numᵃ (4Q23)	DJD 12:168	Of no textual value.
Num 9:3-10 (v. 9 N/R)	4QLev-Numᵃ (4Q23)	DJD 12:168	Fragmentary; identical to MT except scribal error ביום for בין v. 1.
Num 9:15-10:3 (9:16 N/R; 3 letters 9:19; 9:20-21 N/R; 10:1 N/R)	4Q365	DJD 13:303-304	Very fragmentary; mostly follows MT.
Num 9:19-20	4QLev-Numᵃ (4Q23)	DJD 12:168	Identical to MT.
Num 10:9	1QM 10:6-8	*DSSHU* 25	Generally follows MT; most non-MT readings are unique.
Num 10:13-23 (1 letter v. 15; v. 20 N/R)	4QLev-Numᵃ (4Q23)	DJD 12:169	Fragmentary; follows MT.
Num 11:4-5	4QLev-Numᵃ (4Q23)	DJD 12:169	Of no textual value.
Num 11:16-22 (1 letter v. 16)	4QLev-Numᵃ (4Q23)	DJD 12:169-170	Very fragmentary; identical to MT.
Num 11:31-12:11 (12:7 N/R; 1 letter 12:11)	4QNumᵇ (4Q27)	DJD 12:216	Several LXX and unique readings; note orthographic variant מואדה for מאד 11:34.
Num 12:3-11	4QLev-Numᵃ (4Q23)	DJD 12:170	Fragmentary; follows MT.
Num 13:7-24 (vv. 8-9, 14 N/R)	4QNumᵇ (4Q27)	DJD 12:218-219	Fragmentary; generally follows LXX and/or Sam.
Num 13:12-25	4Q365	DJD 13:305	Puts v. 13 after v. 15; a confusing array of readings.
Num 13:21	4QLev-Numᵃ (4Q23)	DJD 12:170	לבא חֻ

Reference	*Scroll*	*Location*	*Comments*
Num 13:29-30	4Q365	DJD 13:307	Very fragmentary; follows MT.
Num 14:16-20	4Q364	DJD 13:224-225	Fragmentary; generally follows MT; unknown addition after v. 20.
Num 15:26-28	4Q365	DJD 13:308	Very fragmentary; follows MT.
Num 15:41-16:11 (4 letters 15:41)	4QNum^b (4Q27)	DJD 12:220-221	Fragmentary; a mixed array of readings.
Num 16:14-16	4QNum^b (4Q27)	DJD 12:221	Extremely fragmentary; identical to MT.
Num 17:12-17 (1 letter v. 16)	4QNum^b (4Q27)	DJD 12:222	Follows MT.
Num 17:20-24	4Q365	DJD 13:309	Follows MT.
Num 18:25-19:6 (2 letters 18:25)	4QNum^b (4Q27)	DJD 12:223	Generally follows MT with a few notable exceptions.
Num 19:19	4Q394	DJD 10:48	Paraphrase of no textual value.
Num 20:7-8	5/6 HevNum (5/6 Hev1a)	Yadin, *IEJ* 12:229	למשה לאמר קח את המטה Identical to MT.
Num 20:12-13b (1 letter v. 12; 3 letters v. 13a)	4QNum^b (4Q27)	DJD 12:225	Sam addition taken from Deut chaps. 3 & 2.
Num 20:16-21:2 (1 letter 20:16; 20:18 N/R; 1 letter 21:2)	4QNum^b (4Q27)	DJD 12:226-227	Part of 20:18 duplicated in 20:20; otherwise follows MT.
Num 20:17-18	4Q364	DJD 13:230	Inserted before Deut 2:8 (=Sam); follows Sam.
Num 21:12a-13a	4QNum^b (4Q27)	DJD 12:228	Consists primarily of Sam additions taken from Deut 2.
Num 21:18	4Q266	DJD 18:41	2 letters; of no textual value.
Num 21:18	4Q267	DJD 18:97	Follows MT.

Reference	Scroll	Location	Comments
Num 22:5-6	4QLev-Num[a] (4Q23)	DJD 12:171	Very fragmentary; identical to MT.
Num 22:5-21	4QNum[b] (4Q27)	DJD 12:230-231	Generally follows LXX.
Num 22:22-24	4QLev-Num[a] (4Q23)	DJD 12:171	Fragmentary; follows MT.
Num 22:31-34	4QNum[b] (4Q27)	DJD 12:231	Fragmentary; most non-MT readings are unique.
Num 22:37-38	4QNum[b] (4Q27)	DJD 12:234	אמנם יכֻל
Num 22:41-23:6 (1 letter 23:6)	4QNum[b] (4Q27)	DJD 12:234	Includes LXX interpolation; mostly follows LXX or Sam.
Num 23:13-15	4QNum[b] (4Q27)	DJD 12:234	Very fragmentary; follows MT.
Num 23:21-22	4QNum[b] (4Q27)	DJD 12:235	א ראה יֶם Of no textual value.
Num 23:27-24:10	4QNum[b] (4Q27)	DJD 12:235-236	Fragmentary; generally follows MT with many unique readings.
Num 24:15-17	4QTest (4Q175)	DJD 5:58	Text complete; prone to paraphrase; of little textual value.
Num 24:17	4Q266	DJD 18:52	וגלחו את הרוש for MT והתגלח, otherwise follows MT.
Num 24:17	4Q269	DJD 18:128	ךְ כוכב מָ
Num 24:17-19	1QM 11:5-7	*DSSHU* plate 26	Scrambled, partial quote with many odd variants.
Num 25:4-8	4QNum[b] (4Q27)	DJD 12:237	Fragmentary; follows MT.

Reference	*Scroll*	*Location*	*Comments*
Num 25:16-26:3 (25:19 N/R)	4QNum[b] (4Q27)	DJD 12:237-238	Fragmentary; follows MT except formulaic LXX addition 25:16.
Num 26:5-7	4QLev-Num[a] (4Q23)	DJD 12:171	Fragmentary; follows MT.
Num 26:4-34 (vv.6, 11, 13 N/R)	4QNum[b] (4Q27)	DJD 12:239-240	Fragmentary; sometimes follows MT, sometimes LXX, sometimes Sam, several unique readings.
Num 26:62-64	4QNum[b] (4Q27)	DJD 12:242	Fragmentary; follows MT.
Num 26:64-27:10 (27:6, 9 N/R)	4QNum[b] (4Q27)	DJD 12:242-243	Mostly follows MT.
Num 27:11	4Q365	DJD 13:310	Extremely fragmentary; follows MT.
Num 27:18-19	4QNum[b] (4Q27)	DJD 12:243	Of no textual value.
Num 27:21-23b	4QNum[b] (4Q27)	DJD 12:243	Mostly follows MT; includes Sam addition from Deut 3 in v. 23.
Num 28:13-17 (1 word v. 13)	4QNum[b] (4Q27)	DJD 12:246	Mostly follows MT.
Num 28:28-31 (2 letters v. 28; v. 29 N/R)	4QNum[b] (4Q27)	DJD 12:247	Very fragmentary; follows MT.
Num 29:10-13 (2 letters v. 10)	4QNum[b] (4Q27)	DJD 12:247	Average of 1 word per verse; of no textual value.
Num 29:14-24 (1 letter v. 14; v. 15 N/R; 1 letter v. 24)	4Q366	DJD 13:340	Some variance, but tends toward MT-type text. Note that the bracket in the word *vacat* in line 5 is facing the wrong way.
Num 29:16-18 (2 letters v. 16; 1 letter v. 18)	4QNum[b] (4Q27)	DJD 12:247	Extremely fragmentary; v. 17 follows MT.

Reference	Scroll	Location	Comments
Num 29:26-30	4QNum^b (4Q27)	DJD 12:248	Fragmentary; unique addition v. 28; otherwise follows MT.
Num 29:32-30:1	4Q366	DJD 13:341	Follows MT with some word order peculiarities.
Num 30:1-3	4QNum^b (4Q27)	DJD 12:248	Fragmentary; follows MT.
Num 30:3(?)	4QLev-Num^a (4Q23)	DJD 12:171	Of no textual value.
Num 30:5-9 (1 questionable word v. 5)	4QNum^b (4Q27)	DJD 12:248	Fragmentary; generally follows LXX.
Num 30:7(? 9? 13?)	4QLev-Num^a (4Q23)	DJD 12:172	Of no textual value.
Num 30:15-31:6 (1 letter 30:15; 1 letter 30:17; 31:1 N/R)	4QNum^b (4Q27)	DJD 12:250-251	Fragmentary; follows MT except 2 unique readings.
Num 31:21-25 (1 letter v. 22; 2 letters v. 25)	4QNum^b (4Q27)	DJD 12:251	Fragmentary; generally follows MT.
Num 31:30-38 (vv. 34, 37 N/R; 2 letters v. 38)	4QNum^b (4Q27)	DJD 12:251-252	Generally follows MT.
Num 31:43-47 (v. 45 N/R)	4QNum^b (4Q27)	DJD 12:252	Very fragmentary; follows MT.
Num 31:48-32:1	4QNum^b (4Q27)	DJD 12:253	Generally follows LXX.
Num 32:4-10	4QNum^b (4Q27)	DJD 12:253-254	Fragmentary; follows MT.
Num 32:8-15	4QLev-Num^a (4Q23)	DJD 12:172	Follows MT.
Num 32:13-19 (v. 18 N/R; 2 letters v. 19)	4QNum^b (4Q27)	DJD 12:254	Very fragmentary; follows MT.

Reference	*Scroll*	*Location*	*Comments*
Num 32:21-30	4QNum[b] (4Q27)	DJD 12:255-256	Fragmentary; includes some expansions from Sam & elsewhere.
Num 32:23-42 (vv. 26, 40 N/R)	4QLev-Num[a] (4Q23)	DJD 12:172-173	Fragmentary; follows MT.
Num 32:35-39 (v. 36 N/R)	4QNum[b] (4Q27)	DJD 12:256	Fragmentary; generally follows MT.
Num 32:41-33:4 (32:42 N/R)	4QNum[b] (4Q27)	DJD 12:256	Fragmentary; follows MT.
Num 33:5-9 (3 letters v. 5; 1 letter v. 9)	4QLev-Num[a] (4Q23)	DJD 12:174	Very fragmentary; follows MT.
Num 33:22-34 (vv. 23-24, 26-27, 29-30, 32 N/R; 1 word v. 34)	4QLev-Num[a] (4Q23)	DJD 12:174	Extremely fragmentary; textual value questionable.
Num 33:23	4QNum[b] (4Q27)	DJD 12:257	תָה
Num 33:25	4QNum[b] (4Q27)	DJD 12:257	יְהֹנוּ
Num 33:28	4QNum[b] (4Q27)	DJD 12:257	רח
Num 33:31	4QNum[b] (4Q27)	DJD 12:257	יסעו
Num 33:31-49 (1 letter v. 32; vv. 34-37 N/R; 3 letters v. 41; v. 43 N/R)	4Q364	DJD 13:225-226	Omits v. 40 (=LXX[mss]); otherwise generally follows MT.
Num 33:45-48 (1 letter v. 45; v. 46 N/R; 2 letters v. 48)	4QNum[b] (4Q27)	DJD 12:258	Of no textual value.
Num 33:47-53	2QNum[b] (2Q7)	DJD 3:58-59	Fragmentary; follows MT except v. 52 omits כל before יושבי.

Reference	Scroll	Location	Comments
Num 33:50-52 (1 letter v. 52)	4QNum[b] (4Q27)	DJD 12:258	Of no textual value.
Num 33:52-54	4QLev-Num[a] (4Q23)	DJD 12:174	Fragmentary; identical to MT.
Num 34:4-9	4QNum[b] (4Q27)	DJD 12:258	Very fragmentary; follows MT.
Num 34:10 (?)	MurNum (Mur1)	DJD 2:78	לכם לְגְבֻ] [קְ
Num 34:19-23 (1 letter v. 20; v. 22 N/R)	4QNum[b] (4Q27)	DJD 12:258	Of no textual value.
Num 35:3-5	4QNum[b] (4Q27)	DJD 12:259	Fragmentary; follows MT.
Num 35:4-5	4QLev-Num[a] (4Q23)	DJD 12:174	Fragmentary; identical to MT.
Num 35:11-15 (1 letter v. 11; v. 13 N/R)	4QNum[b] (4Q27)	DJD 12:259	Very fragmentary; follows MT.
Num 35:18-25 (1 word v. 25)	4QNum[b] (4Q27)	DJD 12:259-260	Several unique readings; 2 LXX expansions.
Num 35:27-28	4QNum[b] (4Q27)	DJD 12:260	Fragmentary; mostly follows MT.
Num 35:33-36:2	4QNum[b] (4Q27)	DJD 12:260	Fragmentary; adds "Eleazar the priest" v. 1 (=LXX); otherwise follows MT.
Num 36:1-2	4Q365	DJD 13:310	Omits וידבר v. 1; otherwise follows MT.
Num 36:4a-7 (1 letter v. 7)	4QNum[b] (4Q27)	DJD 12:262	Includes a lengthy and previously unknown addition v. 4; otherwise mostly follows MT.

Reference	*Scroll*	*Location*	*Comments*
Num 36:7-8 (?)	1QPaleoLev (1Q3)	DJD 1:53	Archaic script; ולא אבותי ת Identical to MT if correct identification.
Num 36:7-11	MurNum (Mur1)	DJD 2:78	Fragmentary; identical to MT.

Deut 1:1	4Q394	DJD 10:46	More allusion than quote.
Deut 1:1-6 (v. 3 N/R)	4Q364	DJD 13:227	Follows MT.
Deut 1:1-17 (1 letter v. 12)	4QDeut^h (4Q35)	DJD 14:63	Follows MT.
Deut 1:4-5	11QDeut (11Q3)	DJD 23:11	Fragmentary; identical to MT.
Deut 1:7-9	2QDeut^a (2Q10)	DJD 3:60	Fragmentary; one reading in v. 8 supports LXX; otherwise it follows MT.
Deut 1:8?	4QpaleoDeut^r (4Q45)	DJD 9:135	Of no textual value.
Deut 1:9-13 (vv. 10, 12 N/R)	1QDeut^b (1Q5)	DJD 1:58	Fragmentary; follows MT.
Deut 1:17-33 (v. 22 N/R; 2 letters v. 23; vv. 29-30 N/R; 1 letter v. 31)	4Q364	DJD 13:228-229	Very fragmentary; generally follows MT with unique addition v. 17.
Deut 1:22-24 (v. 23 N/R; 1 letter v. 24)	4QDeut^h (4Q35)	DJD 14:64	Fragmentary; follows MT.
Deut 1:22-25	1QDeut^a (1Q4)	DJD 1:54	Extremely fragmentary; mostly follows MT.

Reference	Scroll	Location	Comments
Deut 1:29-39 (v. 30, 34 N/R)	4QDeut[h] (4Q35)	DJD 14:64	Very fragmentary; textual nature uncertain.
Deut 1:41	4QDeut[h] (4Q35)	DJD 14:65	ותענו את
Deut 1:43-2:6 (1 word 1:43)	4QDeut[h] (4Q35)	DJD 14:65	Fragmentary; non-MT readings are unique.
Deut 1:45-46	4Q364	DJD 13:230	Very fragmentary; follows MT.
Deut 2:8	4QDeut[o] (4Q42)	DJD 14:130	Very fragmentary; follows MT.
Deut 2:8-14 (vv. 10-11 N/R)	4Q364	DJD 13:230-231	Follows MT.
Deut 2:24-36	4QDeut[d] (4Q31)	*JBL* 112:23-42	Fragmentary; mostly follows MT.
Deut 2:28-30	4QDeut[h] (4Q35)	DJD 14:66	Follows MT.
Deut 2:28-30 (3 letters v. 28; 4 letters v. 30)	11QDeut (11Q3)	DJD 23:12	Very fragmentary; follows MT.
Deut 2:30-3:2	4Q364	DJD 13:232-233	Semi-paraphrase; textual value uncertain.
Deut 3:14-4:1	4QDeut[d] (4Q31)	*JBL* 112:23-42	Fragmentary; mostly follows MT.
Deut 3:18-22	4QDeut[m] (4Q40)	DJD 14:114	Fragmentary; mostly follows MT; adds אלוהיכמה above the line v. 19 (=LXX)
Deut 3:18-23	4Q364	DJD 13:234	Mostly follows MT.
Deut 3:24	4QDeut[e] (4Q32)	DJD 14:40	One partial line; follows MT.
Deut 3:25-26	4QDeut[c] (4Q30)	DJD 14:17	Very fragmentary; identical to MT.
Deut 4:13-17	4QDeut[c] (4Q30)	DJD 14:17	Fragmentary; generally follows MT.
Deut 4:24-26	4QDeut[f] (4Q33)	DJD 14:46	Fragmentary; follows MT.

Reference	Scroll	Location	Comments
Deut 4:30-34 (3 letters vv. 30, 31)	4QDeut° (4Q42)	DJD 14:130	Extremely fragmentary; follows MT.
Deut 4:31-32	4QDeutᶜ (4Q30)	DJD 14:17	Extremely fragmentary; of no textual value.
Deut 4:31-34	4QDeutʰ (4Q35)	DJD 14:66	Fragmentary; follows MT.
Deut 4:32-33	4QDeutᵐ (4Q40)	DJD 14:115	Very fragmentary; reads plural after כַּאֲשֶׁר v. 33.
Deut 4:47, 49	1QDeutᵃ (1Q4)	DJD 1:54	אֲשֶׁר בְּעֵ בֶ הָעֲרָבָה תַּחַת Identification questionable; editors presume a non-MT reading.
Deut 5:1-5 (v. 4 N/R)	4QDeut° (4Q42)	DJD 14:130-131	Very fragmentary; follows MT.
Deut 5:1-11	4QDeutʲ (4Q37)	DJD 14:80	Generally follows MT.
Deut 5:1-14 (vv. 2-9, 11 N/R)	4Qphylᵃ (4Q128)	DJD 6:49	One non-MT reading; prefers LXX.
Deut 5:1-16 (more vv. absent than present)	4Qphyl° (4Q142)	DJD 6:74-75	Very fragmentary; mostly follows MT.
Deut 5:1-21	4Qphylᵍ (4Q134)	DJD 6:59-60	Fairly complete; mostly follows MT.
Deut 5:1-22	1Qphyl (1Q13)	DJD 1:72-73	Several small fragments tentatively pieced together into a smattering of this text. No certain variant from MT.
Deut 5:1-24	4Qphylʲ (4Q137)	DJD 6:65-66	Fairly complete; tends toward LXX.

Reference	Scroll	Location	Comments
Deut 5:1-6:1 (5:30 N/R; 1 letter 6:1)	4QDeutⁿ (4Q41)	DJD 14:123-128	Text nearly complete; some occasional affinities with LXX or Sam; frequently harmonizes to Exod, including expansion in 5:15; otherwise generally follows MT.
Deut 5:1-6:5	4Qphyl^b (4Q129)	DJD 6:52	Fairly complete; wavers between MT and LXX about half and half.
Deut 5:7-24 (many vv. N/R)	4Qphyl^l (4Q139)	DJD 6:70	Somewhat fragmentary; follows MT.
Deut 5:8-9	4QDeut^o (4Q42)	DJD 14:131	Of no solid textual value (see DJD discussion p. 131-132 on possible reconstructions).
Deut 5:13-15	4QDeut^j (4Q37)	DJD 14:81	Fragmentary; follows MT.
Deut 5:21	4QDeut^j (4Q37)	DJD 14:81	Follows MT.
Deut 5:22-28	4QDeut^j (4Q37)	DJD 14:82	Fragmentary; generally follows MT.
Deut 5:22-6:5	4Qphyl^h (4Q135)	DJD 6:61-62	Mostly follows MT.
Deut 5:23-27 (v. 26 N/R)	1Qphyl (1Q13)	DJD 1:74	רבון נוכי ידבר ומתנ אלה Of no textual value.
Deut 5:24-6:3 (6:1 N/R)	4Qphyl^j (4Q137)	DJD 6:66	Fragmentary; mostly follows MT.
Deut 5:27-6:3 (6:1 N/R)	4Qphyl^a (4Q128)	DJD 6:49	Fragmentary; follows MT.
Deut 5:27-6:9	4Qmez^c (4Q151)	DJD 6:82	Very fragmentary; follows MT.
Deut 5:28-29	4QTest (4Q175)	DJD 5:57-58	Mostly follows MT.
Deut 5:28-32 (1 letter v. 32)	4QDeut^{k1} (4Q38)	DJD 14:95	Fragmentary; follows MT (see *BHS* note c-c v. 29).

Reference	Scroll	Location	Comments
Deut 5:29	4QBibPar (4Q158)	DJD 5:3	Small portion of Sam text. Actually Exod 20:21 in Sam.
Deut 5:29-6:3	4QDeut^j (4Q37)	DJD 14:84	Fragmentary; follows MT.
Deut 5:30-31	4QBibPar (4Q158)	DJD 5:3	Small portions of each verse with running paraphrase. Follows MT.
Deut 5:33-6:5	4Qphyl^m (4Q140)	DJD 6:72	Fairly complete; follows every text available at some point, and includes some unique oddities.
Deut 6:4-9	Murphyl (Mur4)	DJD 2:85	Text complete; follows MT.
Deut 6:4-9	4Qphyl^c (4Q130)	DJD 6:55	Follows MT except for two minor LXX readings.
Deut 6:4-11 (3 letters v. 7; 4 letters v. 9)	4QDeut^p (4Q43)	DJD 14:135	Very fragmentary; follows MT.
Deut 6:5-6	4Qmez^b (4Q150)	DJD 6:81	וּבְ מְאֹדֶךָ וְהָיוּ Of no textual value.
Deut 6:5-7	4Qmez^d (4Q152)	DJD 6:83	ךָ וּבְכָל מְאֹד ךָ וְ וְשִׁנַּנְתָּם לְבָ Identical to MT.
Deut 6:6-7 (?)	4Qphyl^i (4Q136)	DJD 6:63	יָ מֹן]ה הָיוּ בְּשִׁבְתְּ Of no textual value.
Deut 6:7-9	4Qphyl^o (4Q142)	DJD 6:74-75	Very fragmentary; two readings favor LXX; one follows Sam; otherwise follows MT.
Deut 7:2-5	4QpaleoDeut^r (4Q45)	DJD 9:135	Fragmentary; וְעָבַד ועבדו for v.4 (=LXX, Sam).
Deut 7:3-4 (3 letters v. 3)	4QDeut^c (4Q30)	DJD 14:18	Adds אלהי[כם after יהוה v. 4.

Reference	Scroll	Location	Comments
Deut 7:6-7 (1 word v.7)	4QpaleoDeut^r (4Q45)	DJD 9:136	Very fragmentary; follows MT.
Deut 7:9	4QCommunal Confession (4Q393)	DJD 29:53	Fragmentary; follows MT except may read לאהֲבָ]יך for MT לאהביו.
Deut 7:12-16	4QDeut^c (4Q32)	DJD 14:40	Fragmentary; identical to MT.
Deut 7:15-24	5QDeut (5Q1)	DJD 3:170	Fairly large fragment with many lacunae; generally follows MT.
Deut 7:16-21	4QpaleoDeut^r (4Q45)	DJD 9:136	Fragmentary; follows MT.
Deut 7:18-22 (3 letters v. 18)	4QDeut^m (4Q40)	DJD 14:116	Fragmentary; an apparent spelling error v. 22; otherwise follows MT.
Deut 7:21-22	1QM (1Q33) 10:1-2	DSSHU plate 25	Loose paraphrase of no textual value.
Deut 7:21-25 (1 letter v. 21)	4QpaleoDeut^r (4Q45)	DJD 9:137	Fragmentary; mostly follows Sam.
Deut 7:21-8:4	4QDeut^c (4Q32)	DJD 14:41	Fragmentary; follows MT except בידך v. 11 (=LXX).
Deut 7:22-25	4QDeut^f (4Q33)	DJD 14:47	Fragmentary; mostly follows MT.
Deut 7:26	4Q397	DJD 10:58	Follows MT
Deut 8:1-5	4QDeut^c (4Q30)	DJD 14:18	Generally follows MT.
Deut 8:2-14	4QDeut^f (4Q33)	DJD 14:47-48	Fragmentary; generally follows MT.
Deut 8:5-7 (1 word v. 6; 1 letter v. 7)	4QDeut^c (4Q32)	DJD 14:42	Of no textual value.

Reference	Scroll	Location	Comments
Deut 8:5-10	4QDeut^j (4Q37)	DJD 14:85	Fragmentary; readings about evenly divided between LXX and MT.
Deut 8:5-10	4QDeut^n (4Q41)	*SWDS* 18, 29-30; DJD 14:122	Mostly follows MT.
Deut 8:5-9:2 (v. 6 N/R)	5QDeut (5Q1)	DJD 3:171	Fragmentary; generally follows MT.
Deut 8:8-9	1QDeut^b (1Q5)	DJD 1:58	מן ו תחצב נח Of no textual value.
Deut 8:10-11	4QDeut^c (4Q32)	DJD 14:43	5 letters total; of no textual value.
Deut 8:15-16	4QDeut^c (4Q32)	DJD 14:43	Of no textual value.
Deut 8:18-19	1QDeut^a (1Q4)	DJD 1:54	הקים תה אחרי Of no textual value
Deut 9:6-7	4Q364	DJD 13:235	Fragmentary; follows MT.
Deut 9:6-7	4QDeut^f (4Q33)	DJD 14:48	Of no textual value.
Deut 9:10	1QDeut^b (1Q5)	DJD 1:58	באצבע אלה]ים[Of no textual value.
Deut 9:11-12	4QDeut^c (4Q30)	DJD 14:19	אלי ה אלי אשר Of no textual value.
Deut 9:12-14	4QDeut^g (4Q34)	*JBL* 112:23-42	Very fragmentary; identical to MT
Deut 9:12-18	4Q364	DJD 13:236	Readings about evenly split between MT and LXX.
Deut 9:17-19	4QDeut^c (4Q30)	DJD 14:19	Very fragmentary; follows MT.
Deut 9:22-24	4Q364	DJD 13:237	Fragmentary; follows MT.

Reference	Scroll	Location	Comments
Deut 9:27-28	1QDeut^a (1Q4)	DJD 1:54	קוב ר יוצאנ Of no textual value.
Deut 9:27-29 (3 letters v. 27)	4Q364	DJD 13:238	Fragmentary; follows MT.
Deut 9:29-10:2 (1 letter 9:29)	4QDeut^c (4Q30)	DJD 14:19	A couple of curious scribal errors; otherwise of no textual value.
Deut 10:1-3	MurDeut (Mur2)	DJD 2:79	Fragmentary; identical to MT.
Deut 10:1-4 (include 9:21 and 25?)	4Q364	DJD 13:239	9:21? And 25? Are more likely commentary; 10:1-4 has several unique readings.
Deut 10:5-8 (2 letters v. 8)	4QDeut^c (4Q30)	DJD 14:20	Fragmentary; follows MT.
Deut 10:6-7(?)	4Q364	DJD 13:240	Paraphrase?
Deut 10:8-12	2QDeut^c (2Q12)	DJD 3:61	Fragmentary, follows MT.
Deut 10:10-13 (1 letter v. 13)	4Q364	DJD 13:241	Possible commentary near v. 3 makes textual character uncertain.
Deut 10:11-12 (2 uncertain letters v. 11)	4QpaleoDeut^r (4Q45)	DJD 9:138	Very fragmentary; identical to MT.
Deut 10:12-15	4QDeut^l (4Q39)	DJD 14:110	Extremely fragmentary; follows MT.
Deut 10:12-20	4Qmez^c (151)	DJD 6:82	Very fragmentary; follows MT.
Deut 10:12-11:12	4Qphyl^k (4Q138)	DJD 6:68-69	Fairly complete; markedly prefers LXX.
Deut 10:12-11:17 (many portions N/R)	4Qphyl^a (4Q128)	DJD 6:49-50	Very fragmentary; tends toward LXX.

Reference	*Scroll*	*Location*	*Comments*
Deut 10:12-11:21	8Qmez (8Q4)	DJD 3:158-160	Extremely fragmentary; departs from MT frequently toward other types of text.
Deut 10:14-11:2 (many vv. N/R)	4Qmez[b] (150)	DJD 6:81	Fragmentary; mostly follows MT.
Deut 10:17-18	1Qphyl (1Q13)	DJD 1:74	Extremely fragmentary; follows MT.
Deut 10:21-11:1, 8-11, 12	1Qphyl (1Q13)	DJD 1:74-75	Three fragments; follows MT.
Deut 10:22-11:2 (2 letters 10:22; 2 letters 11:2)	4Q364	DJD 13:242	Of no textual value.
Deut 10:22-11:3 (most of 11:1-2 N/R)	4Qphyl[p] (4Q143)	DJD 6:75	Fragmentary; follows MT.
Deut 11:2-3	MurDeut (Mur2)	DJD 2:79	Fragmentary; identical to MT.
Deut 11:3	4QDeut[c] (4Q30)	DJD 14:20	Extremely fragmentary; follows MT.
Deut 11:4	4QLXXDeut (4Q122)	DJD 9:195	Very fragmentary; identical to LXX.
Deut 11:4-18 (vv. 5-12, 14-15 N/R)	4Qphyl[q] (4Q144)	DJD 6:76	Fragmentary; mostly illegible; follows MT.
Deut 11:6-9	4Q364	DJD 13:242	Semi-paraphrase; most readings are unique.
Deut 11:6-13 (2 letters v. 11)	4QDeut[j] (4Q37)	DJD 14:86	Fragmentary; most readings are unique.
Deut 11:6-13	4QDeut[k1] (4Q38)	DJD 14:96	Generally follows MT.
Deut 11:9-13	4QDeut[c] (4Q30)	DJD 14:21	Fragmentary; follows MT.
Deut 11:10 (?)	6QDeut (?) (6Q20)	DJD 3:136	Identification tenuous.

Reference	Scroll	Location	Comments
Deut 11:13-21	Murphyl (Mur4)	DJD 2:83-84	Text complete; follows MT nearly to the letter.
Deut 11:13-21	4Qphyl^a (4Q128)	DJD 6:55	Follows MT.
Deut 11:13-21 (vv. 15, 18, 20 N/R; one certain letter of v. 14)	4Qphyl^d (4Q131)	DJD 6:56	Of no textual value.
Deut 11:13-21 (vv. 14, 19, 20 N/R)	4Qphylⁱ (4Q136)	DJD 6:63	Fragmentary; follows MT.
Deut 11:17-18	4Qmez^e (4Q153)	DJD 6:83	בולה ברי אלה עֵינֵיכֶם Of no textual value.
Deut 11:18	4QDeut^c (4Q30)	DJD 14:21	Fragmentary; follows MT.
Deut 11:18-21	4Qphyl^a (4Q128)	DJD 6:50	Very fragmentary; follows MT.
Deut 11:18-21	4Qphyl^p (4Q143)	DJD 6:75-76	Fragmentary; follows MT.
Deut 11:19-21	4Qphyl^s (4Q146)	DJD 6:79	Fairly complete on a narrow strip; follows MT.
Deut 11:21 (?)	4QDeut^j (4Q37)	DJD 14:88	יְהוָה
Deut 11:23-24	4Q364	DJD 13:243	Very fragmentary; identical to MT.
Deut 11:27-30	1QDeut^a (1Q4)	DJD 1:55	Very fragmentary; follows MT.
Deut 11:28	4QpaleoDeut^r (4Q45)	DJD 9:138	Very fragmentary; identical to MT.
Deut 11:30-31	1QDeut^b (1Q5)	DJD 1:58	לא עֲרָבָה מו את Of no textual value.
Deut 11:30-12:1	4QpaleoDeut^r (4Q45)	DJD 9:138	Fragmentary; follows MT except ואל]ה 12:1 (=LXX).

Reference	*Scroll*	*Location*	*Comments*
Deut 12:2-5 (v. 4 N/R)	4QpaleoDeut^r (4Q45)	DJD 9:139	Follows MT except מצבותיהם v. 3 (=Sam).
Deut 12:5	4Q394	DJD 10:50	Semi-paraphrase; reads בחר for MT יבחר.
Deut 12:11-12 (1 letter v. 12)	4QpaleoDeut^r (4Q45)	DJD 9:139	Very fragmentary; identical to MT.
Deut 12:18-19	4QDeut^c (4Q30)	DJD 14:22	Very fragmentary; 1 MT and 1 LXX reading.
Deut 12:22	4QpaleoDeut^r (4Q45)	DJD 9:139	א[ת הצבי וא[ת
Deut 12:25-26	MurDeut (Mur2)	DJD 2:79	Only a few letters; identical to MT.
Deut 12:26	4QDeut^c (4Q30)	DJD 14:22	ך תשא ב Of no textual value.
Deut 12:31	4QDeut^c (4Q30)	DJD 14:22	שנא Of no textual value.
Deut 13:1-4, 4-6	1QDeut^a (1Q4)	DJD 1:55	Most readings uncertain.
Deut 13:5	4QDeut^c (4Q30)	DJD 14:22	Extremely fragmentary; 1 Sam reading.
Deut 13:7	4QDeut^c (4Q30)	DJD 14:23	Very fragmentary; apparently several scribal errors.
Deut 13:7-11	11QTemple^b (11Q20)	DJD 23:401	Very fragmentary; generally follows LXX.
Deut 13:11-12	4QDeut^c (4Q30)	DJD 14:23	Very fragmentary; follows MT.
Deut 13:13-14	1QDeut^a (1Q4)	DJD 1:55	Very fragmentary; follows MT.
Deut 13:16	4QDeut^c (4Q30)	DJD 14:23	ואת בהמתה
Deut 13:19-14:1 (1 letter 14:1)	4QpaleoDeut^r (4Q45)	DJD 9:140	Very fragmentary; adds ו[הטוב 13:19 (=LXX, Sam).
Deut 14:2-4 (v. 3 N/R)	4QpaleoDeut^r (4Q45)	DJD 9:140	Extremely fragmentary; follows MT.

Reference	Scroll	Location	Comments
Deut 14:14-21 (vv. 17, 19 N/R)	4Q366	DJD 13:342	Very fragmentary; mostly follows MT.
Deut 14:19-22 (v. 20 N/R)	4QpaleoDeut^r (4Q45)	DJD 9:141	Fragmentary; only variant from MT is unique.
Deut 14:24-25	1QDeut^a (1Q4)	DJD 1:56	Fragmentary; follows MT.
Deut 14:24-26	4Q364	DJD 13:243	Very fragmentary; mostly follows MT.
Deut 14:26-29 (2 letters v. 29)	4QpaleoDeut^r (4Q45)	DJD 9:141	Fragmentary; follows MT.
Deut 14:29-15:1 or 2	MurDeut (Mur2)	DJD 2:79	אשר שמטה Of no textual value.
Deut 15:1-4	4QDeut^c (4Q30)	DJD 14:24	Fragmentary; follows MT except omission after יגש v. 2 (=LXX).
Deut 15:2	11QMelch (11Q13) 3	van der Woude *OTS* 14: 358	[ש כול בעל משה יד אשר ישה שמטה [. . .] Follows MT except MT reads ידו.
Deut 15:5-6	4QpaleoDeut^r (4Q45)	DJD 9:142	Very fragmentary; identical to MT.
Deut 15:8-10	4QpaleoDeut^r (4Q45)	DJD 9:142	Omits את before ידך v 8 (=Sam), otherwise follows MT.
Deut 15:14-15	1QDeut^b (1Q5)	DJD 1:58	[א[דני א[להי[ך תתן לו ו נכי מצוך לעש MT has יהוה for [א[דני.
Deut 15:15-19	4QDeut^c (4Q30)	DJD 14:24	Fragmentary; mostly follows MT.

Reference	Scroll	Location	Comments
Deut 16:2-3 (3 questionable letters v. 2)	4QDeut^c (4Q30)	DJD 14:25	Of no textual value.
Deut 16:4, 6-7	1QDeut^a (1Q4)	DJD 1:56	Fragmentary; follows MT.
Deut 16:6-11	4QDeut^c (4Q30)	DJD 14:25	Fragmentary; most readings are unique.
Deut 16:13-14	4Q366	DJD 13:341	Follows MT.
Deut 16:21-17:5	4QDeut^c (4Q30)	DJD 14:26	Fragmentary; follows MT.
Deut 17:7	4QDeut^c (4Q30)	DJD 14:27	בראש רבך Follows MT.
Deut 17:12-15 (v. 13 N/R)	2QDeut^b (2Q11)	DJD 3:61	Tiny fragment; follows MT.
Deut 17:15-18:1	4QDeut^c (4Q30)	DJD 14:27	Fragmentary; mostly follows MT.
Deut 17:17-18 (?)	4QDeut^f (4Q33)	DJD 14:49	Of no textual value.
Deut 18:6-10	4QDeut^f (4Q33)	DJD 14:49	Fragmentary; follows MT.
Deut 18:18-19	4QTest (4Q175)	DJD 5:58	Follows MT, except adds הנבי (= הנביא, LXX) in v. 19 before בשמי; many odd spellings.
Deut 18:18-20, 22	4QBibPar (4Q158)	DJD 5:3	Fragmentary; generally follows MT.
Deut 18:18-22	4QDeut^f (4Q33)	DJD 14:49	Fragmentary; follows MT.
Deut 19:2-3	4QpaleoDeut^r (4Q45)	DJD 9:143	Fragmentary; identical to MT.
Deut 19:8-16 (v. 12 N/R; 3 letters v. 16)	4QDeut^{k2} (4Q38a)	DJD 14:101	Fragmentary; textual character uncertain.

Reference	*Scroll*	*Location*	*Comments*
Deut 19:17-20:6 (4 letters 19:17; 20:4 N/R?)	4QDeut^f (4Q33)	DJD 14:50	Mostly follows MT.
Deut 19:20-20:1	4Q365	DJD 13:311	Several scribal errors; generally follows MT.
Deut 19:21 (?)	4QDeut^h (4Q35)	DJD 14:67	Identification uncertain.
Deut 20:2-5	1QM (1Q33) 10:2-5	*DSSHU* plate 25	Free paraphrase of no textual value.
Deut 20:6-19 (2 letters v. 16)	4QDeut^{k2} (4Q38a)	DJD 14:101-102	Fragmentary; mostly follows MT.
Deut 20:9-13	4QDeutⁱ (4Q36)	DJD 14:72	Fragmentary; follows MT.
Deut 21:4-12 (3 letters v. 12)	4QDeut^f (4Q33)	DJD 14:50-51	Mostly follows MT.
Deut 21:8-9	1QDeut^b (1Q5)	DJD 1:58	Fragmentary; follows MT.
Deut 21:23-22:9 (no certain letters 21:23; 1 letter 22:2; 1 letter 22:7; 1 letter 22:9)	4QDeutⁱ (4Q36)	DJD 14:72	Very fragmentary; follows MT.
Deut 22:3-6 (4 letters v. 3)	4QpaleoDeut^r (4Q45)	DJD 9:143	Fragmentary; follows MT.
Deut 22:9	4QInstruction^d (4Q418)	DJD 34:329	Loose allusion of no textual value.
Deut 22:10	4QInstruction^d (4Q418)	DJD 34:329	Extremely fragmentary; identical to MT.
Deut 22:11	4QInstruction^d (4Q418)	DJD 34:329	Of no textual value.
Deut 22:12-19	4QDeut^f (4Q33)	DJD 14:51	Fragmentary; mostly follows MT.
Deut 23:6-8 (2 letters v. 8)	4QDeutⁱ (4Q36)	DJD 14:73	Very fragmentary; follows MT.

Reference	*Scroll*	*Location*	*Comments*
Deut 23:7	4QpaleoDeut^r (4Q45)	DJD 9:144	אִ תדרוש
Deut 23:12-15	4QpaleoDeut^r (4Q45)	DJD 9:144	Very fragmentary; 1 Sam reading, 1 possible unique reading.
Deut 23:12-16	4QDeut^i (4Q36)	DJD 14:73	Fragmentary; follows MT.
Deut 23:18-20	4QDeut^g (4Q34)	*JBL* 112:23-42	Very fragmentary; identical to MT.
Deut 23:21-26	4QDeut^f (4Q33)	DJD 14:52	Fragmentary; identical to MT.
Deut 23:22-24:3	4QDeut^k2 (4Q38a)	DJD 14:102-103	Very fragmentary; follows MT with 1 unique harmonization.
Deut 23:23-26	4QDeut^i (4Q36)	DJD 14:74	Follows MT; DJD says it goes to 24:1, but there is only 1 unidentified letter remaining of 24:1.
Deut 23:26-24:8	4QDeut^a (4Q28)	*JBL* 112:23-42	Fragmentary; generally follows MT except omits מביתו ויצאה 24:2 (=LXX).
Deut 23:24	4Q271	DJD 18:178	Reads להקים for MT ועשית.
Deut 24:2-7	4QDeut^f (4Q33)	DJD 14:52	Fragmentary; follows MT.
Deut 24:10-16 (v. 12 N/R)	1QDeut^b (1Q5)	DJD 1:58	Fragmentary; generally follows MT.
Deut 24:16-22	4QDeut^g (4Q34)	*JBL* 112:23-42	Very fragmentary; identical to MT.
Deut 25:1-5 (v. 4 N/R)	4QDeut^g (4Q34)	*JBL* 112:23-42	Very fragmentary; identical to MT.
Deut 25:3-9	4QDeut^f (4Q33)	DJD 14:53	Fragmentary; identical to MT.

Reference	Scroll	Location	Comments
Deut 25:13-18 (vv. 14, 17 N/R)	1QDeut[b] (1Q5)	DJD 1:59	Fragmentary; of no textual value.
Deut 25:14-26:5 (1 letter of 26:1)	4QDeut[g] (4Q34)	*JBL* 112:23-42	Very fragmentary; identical to MT.
Deut 25:19-26:5 (3 letters 25:19; 1 letter 26:5)	4QDeut[k2] (4Q38a)	DJD 14:103	Fragmentary; follows MT with some odd spellings and other unique peculiarities.
Deut 26:14-15	4QpaleoDeut[s] (4Q46)	DJD 9:154	Very fragmentary; identical to MT.
Deut 26:18-27:10	4QDeut[f] (4Q33)	DJD 14:53	Fragmentary; mostly follows MT.
Deut 26:18-27:1 (?)	4QDeut[k2] (4Q38a)	DJD 14:104	Of no textual value.
Deut 26:19 (?)	6QDeut (6Q20)	DJD 3:107	Five certain letters
Deut 26:19-27:2	4QDeut[c] (4Q30)	DJD 14:28	Fragmentary; mostly follows LXX.
Deut 27:18	4Q271	DJD 18:175	Fragmentary; follows MT.
Deut 27:24-28:7 (1 letter 27:24)	4QDeut[c] (4Q30)	DJD 14:28-29	Fragmentary; mostly follows MT.
Deut 28:8-11	4QDeut[c] (4Q30)	DJD 14:29	Very fragmentary; only listed variant from MT is a reconstruction.
Deut 28:12-14	4QDeut[c] (4Q30)	DJD 14:30	Fragmentary; reads ‫[מצ]ו‬ ‫ך‬ for MT ‫מצוה‬ ‫אתכם‬ v. 14 (=LXX, Sam).
Deut 28:15-18	4QDeut[o] (4Q42)	DJD 14:132	Fragmentary; follows MT.
Deut 28:15-20 (v. 19 omitted)	4QpaleoDeut[r] (4Q45)	DJD 9:145	Deliberately omits v. 19; other readings tend toward LXX[mss] text.
Deut 28:20	4QDeut[c] (4Q30)	DJD 14:30	Of no textual value.

Reference	*Scroll*	*Location*	*Comments*
Deut 28:21-24	4QDeutᵍ (4Q34)	*JBL* 112:23-42	Very fragmentary; identical to MT; note bracketing typo p. 41.
Deut 28:22-25	4QDeutᶜ (4Q30)	DJD 14:30	Fragmentary; generally follows MT.
Deut 28:27-29	4QDeutᵍ (4Q34)	*JBL* 112:23-42	Very fragmentary; identical to MT
Deut 28:29-30	4QDeutᶜ (4Q30)	DJD 14:31	Fragmentary; follows MT.
Deut 28:33-36 (v. 34 N/R)	4QDeutᵒ (4Q42)	DJD 14:132	Extremely fragmentary; follows MT.
Deut 28:44-48	1QDeutᵇ (1Q5)	DJD 1:59	Very fragmentary; follows MT.
Deut 28:47-52	4QDeutᵒ (4Q42)	DJD 14:133	Fragmentary; follows MT.
Deut 28:48-50 (4 letters v. 50)	4QDeutᶜ (4Q30)	DJD 14:31	Very fragmentary; follows MT.
Deut 28:58-62 (v. 60 N/R)	4QDeutᵒ (4Q42)	DJD 14:133	Very fragmentary; follows MT.
Deut 28:61	4QDeutᶜ (4Q30)	DJD 14:31	כָּל מכה Of no textual value.
Deut 28:67-68	4QDeutˡ (4Q39)	DJD 14:111	יך אֹ שֶׁר אמָ
Deut 29:2-5	4QDeutˡ (4Q39)	DJD 14:111	Fragmentary; follows MT except לו for לֹא v. 4.
Deut 29:9-20	1QDeutᵇ (1Q5)	DJD 1:59	Fragmentary; generally follows MT with some deviation to Sam.
Deut 29:17-19 (1 letter v. 17)	4QDeutᶜ (4Q30)	DJD 14:32	Very fragmentary; follows MT with 1 unique reading.
Deut 29:24-27 (v. 26 N/R)	4QDeutᵇ (4Q29)	DJD 14:10	Very fragmentary; only variant is uncertain.
Deut 30:1-3	4Q398	DJD 10:59	Paraphrase of no textual value.

Reference	Scroll	Location	Comments
Deut 30:3-14	4QDeut^b (4Q29)	DJD 14:10-11	Very fragmentary; generally follows LXX.
Deut 30:16-18 (2 uncertain letters v. 16)	4QDeut^{k3} (4Q38b)	DJD 14:107	Very fragmentary; follows MT.
Deut 30:19-31:13 (v. 11 N/R)	1QDeut^b (1Q5)	DJD 1:59-60	Fragmentary; mostly follows MT.
Deut 31:9-11	4QDeut^h (4Q35)	DJD 14:67	Very fragmentary; only variant follows LXX.
Deut 31:9-17 (v. 13 N/R; 2 letters v. 14)	4QDeut^b (4Q29)	DJD 14:12	Very fragmentary; generally follows MT.
Deut 31:12	4QDeut^l (4Q39)	DJD 14:111	יְהוה [ ] הָם ושמְ
Deut 31:16-19	4QDeut^c (4Q30)	DJD 14:32	Virtually every text-form is represented in this fragment.
Deut 31:24-32:3	4QDeut^b (4Q29)	DJD 14:13	31:28 is corrupt; generally follows MT.
Deut 31:29	4QpaleoDeut^r (4Q45)	DJD 9:146	Of no textual value.
Deut 32:3	4QDeut^c (4Q30)	DJD 14:33	הב Of no textual value.
Deut 32:6-8 (1 word v. 6; 1 partial word v. 8)	4QpaleoDeut^r (4Q45)	DJD 9:146	Very fragmentary; follows MT.
Deut 32:7-8	4QDeut^j (4Q37)	DJD 14:90	Very fragmentary; reads אלוהים for ישראל v. 8 (=LXX)
Deut 32:10-11 (1 word v. 11)	4QpaleoDeut^r (4Q45)	DJD 9:146	Extremely fragmentary; of no textual value.
Deut 32:13-14	4QpaleoDeut^r (4Q45)	DJD 9:147	Very fragmentary; identical to MT.

Reference	Scroll	Location	Comments
Deut 32:14-20, 32-33	4Qphyl[n] (4Q141)	DJD 6:73-74	Fragmentary; mostly follows LXX.
Deut 32:17-18 (2 letters v. 18)	4QDeut[kl] (4Q38)	DJD 14:97	Extremely fragmentary; follows MT.
Deut 32:17-29	1QDeut[b] (1Q5)	DJD 1:60	Of no textual value; condition too poor to be read accurately.
Deut 32:22-23 (3 letters v. 23)	4QDeut[kl] (4Q38)	DJD 14:97	Very fragmentary; follows MT.
Deut 32:25-27	4QDeut[kl] (4Q38)	DJD 14:98	Very fragmentary; follows MT.
Deut 32:33-35 (v. 34 N/R)	4QpaleoDeut[r] (4Q45)	DJD 9:147	יינם ור לי.
Deut 32:37-43	4QDeut[q] (4Q44)	Skehan, *BASOR* 136: 12-15	Fragmentary; about evenly divided between MT and LXX.
Deut 32:46	4QJubilees[a] (4Q216)	DJD 13:5	Uses singular pronouns for MT plurals.
Deut 33:1-2	4QDeut[l] (4Q39)	DJD 14:112	Extremely fragmentary; follows MT.
Deut 33:2-8 (v. 4 N/R)	4QpaleoDeut[r] (4Q45)	DJD 9:148	Very fragmentary; some unique readings.
Deut 33:8-11	4QTest (4Q175)	DJD 5:58	Text complete; supports LXX a lot, with some indecipherable readings.
Deut 33:8-11, 12 (?), 19-21	4QFlor (4Q174)	DJD 3:56-57	Extremely fragmentary; seems to include pesher; follows MT. Fragmentary; generally follows LXX with many unique readings.
Deut 33:8-22	4QDeut[h] (4Q35)	DJD 14:68	Somewhat fragmentary; a wide array of readings, but leans toward LXX.

Reference	Scroll	Location	Comments
Deut 33:12-24 (v. 20 N/R)	1QDeut^b (1Q5)	DJD 1:61	Fragmentary; follows MT except omits v. 15 (due to homoeoarcton).
Deut 33:29-34:1	4QpaleoDeut^r (4Q45)	DJD 9:148	Extremely fragmentary; 1 unique reading, 1 Vulgate reading.
Deut 34:4-6	4QDeut^l (4Q39)	DJD 14:112	Extremely fragmentary; follows MT except וק[קברו v. 6 (=LXX).
Deut 34:8	4QApocryphon of Josh^a (4Q378)	DJD 22:254	Includes explanatory gloss; otherwise follows MT.

Reference	Scroll	Location	Comments
Josh 2:11-12	4QJosh^b (4Q48)	DJD 14:154	6 letters v. 12, including an apparent ר that ends first word of the verse; otherwise identical to MT.
Josh 2:23(?)	4Q522	DJD 25:42	Identification uncertain.
Josh 3:15-4.3 (4:1 N/R)	4QJosh^b (4Q48)	DJD 14:155	Very poorly preserved; generally follows MT where text and reconstructions are certain.
Josh 5:2-7	4QJosh^a (4Q47)	DJD 14:147	Very fragmentary; ראות for MT הראותם v. 6 (=LXX).
Josh 6:5-10	4QJosh^a (4Q47)	DJD 14:148	Very fragmentary; follows MT with a couple of unique readings.
Josh 6:26	4QTest (4Q175)	DJD 5:58	Loose paraphrase; reads שיש for MT האיש לפני יהוה.

Reference	Scroll	Location	Comments
Josh 7:12-17	4QJosh^a (4Q47)	DJD 14:149	Text is riddled with grammatical and scribal errors; omits משפחה section of v. 14; non-unique readings follow LXX.
Josh 8:3-14 (v. 12-13 N/R)	4QJosh^a (4Q47)	DJD 14:150	Very fragmentary; אל העיר for MT לעיר v. 4; some readings are unique, others follow LXX.
Josh 8:18 (?)	4QJosh^a (4Q47)	DJD 14:150	Position in MS uncertain; of no textual value.
Josh 8:34-35	4QJosh^a (4Q47)	DJD 14:147	1 word v. 34; several unique readings; an unknown passage follows, then biblical text continues with 5:2ff.
Josh 10:2-5	4QJosh^a (4Q47)	DJD 14:151	Fragmentary; omits בני v. 4.
Josh 10:8-11	4QJosh^a (4Q47)	DJD 14:151	Fragmentary; הלך for עלה v. 9; omits גדלות v. 11; otherwise follows MT.
Josh 17:1-5 (3 letters v. 5)	4QJosh^b (4Q48)	DJD 14:158	Very fragmentary; identical to MT.
Josh 17:11-15	4QJosh^b (4Q48)	DJD 14:158-159	Fragmentary; generally follows MT though text appears corrupt in some places.
Judg 6:2-6	4QJudg^a (4Q49)	DJD 14:162	Omits ועלו עליו v. 3; skips from v. 6 to v. 11; otherwise mostly follows MT.
Judg 6:11-13	4QJudg^a (4Q49)	DJD 14:162	Fragmentary; several unique readings.
Judg 6:20-22	1QJudg (1Q6)	DJD 1:62	Fragmentary; identical to MT.

Reference	*Scroll*	*Location*	*Comments*
Judg 8:1 (?)	1QJudg (1Q6)	DJD 1:62	רים מ ת ל]]ל
Judg 9:1-6	1QJudg (1Q6)	DJD 1:62	Fragmentary; follows MT.
Judg 9:28-31	1QJudg (1Q6)	DJD 1:62-63	Fragmentary; textual nature uncertain.
Judg 9:40-43	1QJudg (1Q6)	DJD 1:63	Fragmentary; textual nature uncertain.
Judg 21:12-25	4QJudg^b (4Q50)	DJD 14:166	Very fragmentary; omits אשה end of v. 16; אבותיהם for אבותם v. 22; otherwise follows MT.
Ruth 1:1-6	4QRuth^b (4Q105)	DJD 16:193	Extremely fragmentary; mostly follows MT.
Ruth 1:1-12 (v. 10 N/R)	4QRuth^a (4Q104)	DJD 16:188	Follows MT except וישבו v. 2 (=Syr? *BHS* does not list a variant here) and קולם v 9 (sp?).
Ruth 1:12-15	4QRuth^b (4Q105)	DJD 16:194	Very fragmentary; mostly follows MT.
Ruth 2.13-3.8	2QRuth^a (2Q16)	DJD 3.72-74	Very fragmentary, mostly follows MT.
Ruth 3:13-18	2QRuth^b (2Q17)	DJD 3:74	Fragmentary; mostly follows MT.
Ruth 4:3-4	2QRuth^a (2Q16)	DJD 3:74	מכר ל Of no textual value.

Reference	Scroll	Location	Comments
1 Sam 1:22b-2:6	4QSamᵃ (4Q51)	Cross, *BASOR* 132:15-26	Strikingly similar to LXX against MT.
1 Sam 2:16-25	4QSamᵃ (4Q51)	Cross, *BASOR* 132:15-26	Strikingly similar to LXX.
1 Sam 3:14-17	4QVisSam (4Q160)	DJD 5:9,32	Loose paraphrase of no textual value.
1 Sam 16:1-11 (v. 6 N/R)	4QSamᵇ (4Q52)	Cross, *JBL* 74: 166-172	Fragmentary; tends toward LXX.
1 Sam 18:17-18	1QSam (1Q7)	DJD 1:64	Fragmentary; follows MT.
1 Sam 19:10-17	4QSamᵇ (4Q52)	Cross, *JBL* 74:167	Follows MT, but poor condition makes value questionable.
1 Sam 21:3-10	4QSamᵇ (4Q52)	Cross, *JBL* 74:167-168	Fragmentary; follows MT.
1 Sam 23:9-17	4QSamᵇ (4Q52)	Cross, *JBL* 74:169-171	Extremely fragmentary; of no textual value.
1 Sam 25:30-32	4QSamᶜ (4Q53)	Ulrich, *BASOR* 235:1-25	Very fragmentary; a confusing array of readings.
2 Sam 7:10-14 (Parallel 1 Chr 17:9-13)	4QFlor (4Q174)	DJD 5:53	Loose paraphrase with pesher; of no textual value.
2 Sam 14:7-15:15	4QSamᶜ (4Q53)	Ulrich, *BASOR* 235:1-25	Fragmentary; a confusing array of readings.
2 Sam 20:6-10	1QSam (1Q7)	DJD 1:65	Follows MT; note problem in fragment numbering. DJD lists this as fragment 2; it is actually 2 and 3. The one listed as fragment 3 is actually 4-7.
2 Sam 21:16-18	1QSam (1Q7)	DJD 1:65	See numbering note above. Tends toward wording in Chronicles.
2 Sam 22:6-9 (Psalm 18:6-9)	8QPs (8Q2)	DJD 3:149	Very fragmentary; identical to MT.

Reference	Scroll	Location	Comments
2 Sam 22:10-13 (Psalm 18:10-13)	8QPs (8Q2)	DJD 3:149	Of no textual value.
2 Sam 23:7	11QPsᵃ (11Q5) xxvii	DJD 4:48	ועץ חיצנית ובאש שרף ישרפו בשבת Second word unknown? Otherwise follows MT.
2 Sam 23:9-12	1QSam (1Q7)	DJD 1:65	Somewhat fragmentary; mostly follows MT.
1 Kgs 1:1, 16-17, 27-37 (actual vv. uncertain)	5QKgs (5Q2)	DJD 3:172	Generally follows MT; supports *Qere* in several places.
1 Kgs 3:12-14	6QKgs (6Q4)	DJD 3:107	א הי עשר ך. Of no textual value.
1 Kgs 7:20-21	4QKgs (4Q54)	DJD 14:174	Very fragmentary; identical to MT.
1 Kgs 7:25-27	4QKgs (4Q54)	DJD 14:174	Very fragmentary; identical to MT.
1 Kgs 7:29-31 (4 certain letters v. 29; 2 certain letters v. 31)	4QKgs (4Q54)	DJD 14:174	Very fragmentary; follows MT.
1 Kgs 7:31-42 (v. 36 N/R)	4QKgs (4Q54)	DJD 14:175	Very fragmentary; ממער for MT קצב ;כמער וקצב for MT v. 37; את הסיר (?) for הכיר.
1 Kgs 7:51-8:9 (4 letters 7:51; 8:3 N/R)	4QKgs (4Q54)	DJD 14:176	Fragmentary; לרביר for הלחות 8:6; אל דביר for לחות 8:9; otherwise follows MT.

Reference	*Scroll*	*Location*	*Comments*
1 Kgs 8:16-18	4QKgs (4Q54)	DJD 14:177	Very fragmentary; adds a phrase from 2 Chr 6:5; otherwise mostly follows MT.
1 Kgs 12:28-31	6QKgs (6Q4)	DJD 3:107	Of no textual value.
1 Kgs 22:28-31	6QKgs (6Q4)	DJD 3:108	Fragmentary; generally follows MT.
2 Kgs 2:3-5	4Q382	DJD 13:368	Only preserves a phrase here and there; mostly follows MT.
2 Kgs 2:14-16	4QApocryphe d'Élisée (4Q481a)	DJD 22:307	Some unique readings; partial paraphrase?
2 Kgs 5:26	6QKgs (6Q4)	DJD 3:108	אתך ה ן ובקר
2 Kgs 6:32	6QKgs (6Q4)	DJD 3:108	הראי כבוא אחד Of no textual value.
2 Kgs 7:8-10	6QKgs (6Q4)	DJD 3:109	Identical to MT except one odd spelling.
2 Kgs 7:20-8:5	6QKgs (6Q4)	DJD 3:109	Singularly wild text; value questionable.
2 Kgs 9:1-2	6QKgs (6Q4)	DJD 3:110	השמן ה נמשי ובא Of no textual value.
2 Kgs 20:19-21 (?)	6QKgs (6Q4)	DJD 3:110	Of no textual value.

| 1 Chr 17:9-13 | | | See 2 Sam 7:10-14 |
| 2 Chr 28:27 | 4QChr (4Q118) | DJD 16:296 | Fragmentary; בֶן אחז for MT בנו (unique). |

Reference	Scroll	Location	Comments
2 Chr 29:1-3	4QChr (4Q118)	DJD 16:296	Fragmentary; follows MT with 2 apparent scribal errors.
Ezra 4:2-6 (2 letters v. 2)	4QEzra (4Q117)	DJD 16:292	Very fragmentary; follows MT.
Ezra 4:9-11	4QEzra (4Q117)	DJD 16:292	Fragmentary; follows MT except נהרא for נהרה v. 10; DJD lists this as LXX but it may merely be a question of spelling (see DJD intro p. 291).
Ezra 5:17	4QEzra (4Q117)	DJD 16:292	Very fragmentary; identical to MT.
Ezra 6:1-5	4QEzra (4Q117)	DJD 16:292	Fragmentary; follows MT except ובקר v. 1 (=LXX).
Job 3:5-9 (vv. 7-8 N/R)	4QtgJob (4Q157)	DJD 6:90	הי עננא מי שנה . . . ח Corresponds to MT.
Job 4:16-5:4	4QtgJob (4Q157)	DJD 6:90	Fragmentary; corresponds to MT.
Job 8:15-17 (no legible letters v. 17)	4QJob^b (4Q100)	DJD 16:179	Extremely fragmentary; follows MT.
Job 9:27	4QJob^b (4Q100)	DJD 16:180	שׂצחה שׂיחי
Job 13:4	4QJob^b (4Q100)	DJD 16:180	אׁולם אתם טפלי

Reference	Scroll	Location	Comments
Job 13:18-20	4QpaleoJob^c (4Q101)	DJD 9:156	Of no textual value.
Job 13:23-27	4QpaleoJob^c (4Q101)	DJD 9:156	Extremely fragmentary; follows MT.
Job 14:4-6 (1 letter v. 6)	4QJob^b (4Q100)	DJD 16:180	Very fragmentary; identical to MT.
Job 14:13-18 (1 letter v. 18)	4QpaleoJob^c (4Q101)	DJD 9:156	Extremely fragmentary; only reading is unique.
Job 17:14-18:4	11QtgJob (11Q10)	van der Ploeg, *Le Targum* 12	Very fragmentary; corresponds to MT.
Job 19:11-19 (v. 14 N/R)	11QtgJob (11Q10)	van der Ploeg, *Le Targum* 14	Fragmentary; mostly corresponds to MT.
Job 19:29-20:6	11QtgJob (11Q10)	van der Ploeg, *Le Targum* 16	Fragmentary; corresponds to MT.
Job 21:2-10	11QtgJob (11Q10)	van der Ploeg, *Le Targum* 18	Fragmentary; mostly corresponds to MT (two LXX translations).
Job 21:20-27 (v. 23 omitted?)	11QtgJob (11Q10)	van der Ploeg, *Le Targum* 20	Fragmentary; corresponds to MT except it may omit v. 23.
Job 22:3-9	11QtgJob (11Q10)	van der Ploeg, *Le Targum* 22	Very fragmentary; corresponds to MT.
Job 22:16-22	11QtgJob (11Q10)	van der Ploeg, *Le Targum* 24	Very fragmentary; corresponds to MT.
Job 24:12-17 (v. 15 omitted?)	11QtgJob (11Q10)	van der Ploeg, *Le Targum* 26	Fragmentary; corresponds to MT.
Job 24:24-26:2 (one letter of 26:1)	11QtgJob (11Q10)	van der Ploeg, *Le Targum* 28	Fragmentary; corresponds to MT.
Job 26:10-27:4	11QtgJob (11Q10)	van der Ploeg, *Le Targum* 30	Fragmentary; corresponds to MT.
Job 27:11-20	11QtgJob (11Q10)	van der Ploeg, *Le Targum* 32	Fragmentary; corresponds to MT.

Reference	*Scroll*	*Location*	*Comments*
Job 28:4-13 (v. 12 N/R)	11QtgJob (11Q10)	van der Ploeg, *Le Targum* 34	Scarcely there at all. Of no textual value.
Job 28:20-28	11QtgJob (11Q10)	van der Ploeg, *Le Targum* 36	Fragmentary; corresponds to MT.
Job 29:7-16 (no certain letters of v. 16)	11QtgJob (11Q10)	van der Ploeg, *Le Targum* 38	Fragmentary; corresponds to MT.
Job 29:24-30:4	11QtgJob (11Q10)	van der Ploeg, *Le Targum* 40	Fragmentary; corresponds to MT.
Job 30:13-20	11QtgJob (11Q10)	van der Ploeg, *Le Targum* 42	Somewhat fragmentary; corresponds to MT.
Job 30:25-31:1 (one partial letter of 30:31)	11QtgJob (11Q10)	van der Ploeg, *Le Targum* 44	Very fragmentary; of no textual value.
Job 31:8-16	11QtgJob (11Q10)	van der Ploeg, *Le Targum* 46	No more than two complete words of any verse; corresponds to MT.
Job 31:14-19	4QJob^a (4Q99)	DJD 16:172	Fragmentary; follows MT except reverses עשני and בבטן v. 15 (unique).
Job 31:20-21	4QJob^b (4Q100)	DJD 16:180	Very fragmentary; identical to MT.
Job 31:26-32	11QtgJob (11Q10)	van der Ploeg, *Le Targum* 48	Fragmentary; mostly corresponds to MT.
Job 31:40-32:3	11QtgJob (11Q10)	van der Ploeg, *Le Targum* 50	Fragmentary; corresponds to MT except אדין for *waw* consecutive in 32:2.
Job 32:3-4	4QJob^a (4Q99)	DJD 16:172	Fragmentary; follows MT.
Job 32:10-17	11QtgJob (11Q10)	van der Ploeg, *Le Targum* 52	Fairly complete; corresponds to MT even in some readings that scholars tend to emend.

Reference	Scroll	Location	Comments
Job 33:6-16	11QtgJob (11Q10)	van der Ploeg, *Le Targum* 54	Fairly complete; corresponds to MT.
Job 33:10-11	4QJobª (4Q99)	DJD 16:173	צֵא יחֹש שׁמֹר כֹּל
Job 33:24-30 (v. 27 N/R; 2 letters v. 24; 3 letters v. 28)	4QJobª (4Q99)	DJD 16:173	Very fragmentary; mostly follows MT.
Job 33:24-32	11QtgJob (11Q10)	van der Ploeg, *Le Targum* 56	Somewhat fragmentary; corresponds to MT.
Job 33:28-30	2QJob (2Q15)	DJD 3:71	עָבַר ל פעמים באור הַ Identical to MT.
Job 34:6-17	11QtgJob (11Q10)	van der Ploeg, *Le Targum* 58	Somewhat fragmentary; corresponds to MT.
Job 34:24-34	11QtgJob (11Q10)	van der Ploeg, *Le Targum* 60	Somewhat fragmentary; significantly corresponds to MT.
Job 35:6-15	11QtgJob (11Q10)	van der Ploeg, *Le Targum* 62	Fairly complete; corresponds to MT except one LXX reading v. 11.
Job 35:16	4QJobª (4Q99)	DJD 16:174	בלי דעת מלין י
Job 36:7-11	4QJobª (4Q99)	DJD 16:174	בְכֹסֵא v. 7; DJD lists this as an LXX reading, but LXX εις could reflect either this reading or MT לכסא.
Job 36:7-16	11QtgJob (11Q10)	van der Ploeg, *Le Targum* 64	Fairly complete; corresponds to MT.
Job 36:13-24 (1 letter v. 17)	4QJobª (4Q99)	DJD 16:175	Fragmentary; mostly follows MT but see DJD note on v. 24.

Reference	Scroll	Location	Comments
Job 36:23-33	11QtgJob (11Q10)	van der Ploeg, *Le Targum* 66	Fairly complete; corresponds to MT.
Job 36:25-27	4QJob^a (4Q99)	DJD 16:176	Very fragmentary; וזקן for יזקן v. 27; otherwise follows MT.
Job 36:32-33	4QJob^a (4Q99)	DJD 16:176	אם יגיד רעיו מקנה א
Job 37:1-5	4QJob^a (4Q99)	DJD 16:176	Badly written and badly preserved; several unique readings.
Job 37:10-19	11QtgJob (11Q10)	van der Ploeg, *Le Targum* 68	Nearly complete; corresponds to MT with a few spelling errors.
Job 37:14-15	4QJob^a (4Q99)	DJD 16:177	וך הת תדע בשו
Job 38:3-13	11QtgJob (11Q10)	van der Ploeg, *Le Targum* 70	Nearly complete; corresponds to MT.
Job 38:23-34 (v. 33 N/R)	11QtgJob (11Q10)	van der Ploeg, *Le Targum* 72	Nearly complete; corresponds to MT.
Job 39:1-11	11QtgJob (11Q10)	van der Ploeg, *Le Targum* 74	Nearly complete; corresponds to MT.
Job 39:20-29	11QtgJob (11Q10)	van der Ploeg, *Le Targum* 76	Nearly complete; corresponds to MT, but omits v. 24.
Job 40:5-14	11QtgJob (11Q10)	van der Ploeg, *Le Targum* 78	Nearly complete; corresponds to MT except for a few unique oddities.
Job 40:23-31	11QtgJob (11Q10)	van der Ploeg, *Le Targum* 80	Nearly complete; corresponds to MT.
Job 41:7-17	11QtgJob (11Q10)	van der Ploeg, *Le Targum* 82	Nearly complete; corresponds to MT.

Reference	Scroll	Location	Comments
Job 41:25-42:6 (possibly one letter of 41:25)	11QtgJob (11Q10)	van der Ploeg, *Le Targum* 84	Fairly complete; corresponds to MT.
Job 42:9b-11	11QtgJob (11Q10)	van der Ploeg, *Le Targum* 86	Begins with "God" of v. 9a and ends with "piece of gold" of v. 11; otherwise complete; Ploeg suggests that the scroll ends here, but this is uncertain. Corresponds to MT.

Reference	Scroll	Location	Comments
Ps 1:1a	4QFlor (4Q174)	DJD 5:53-54	Follows MT
Ps 2:1	4QFlor (4Q174)	DJD 5:53-54	Follows MT.
Ps 2:1-8 (1 letter v. 1; 2 letters v. 2; 4 letters v. 8)	11QPs^c (11Q7)	DJD 23:53	Fragmentary; follows MT.
Ps 2:6-7	3QPs (3Q2)	DJD 3:94	ן הר קדשי מר אלי בנ Identical to MT.
Ps 5:8-13 (3 letters v. 8; 4 letters v. 9)	4QPs^s (4Q98b)	DJD 16:154	Very fragmentary; follows MT.
Ps 5:9-6:4	4QPs^a (4Q83)	DJD 16:10	Fragmentary; non-MT readings are unique.
Ps 6:1	4QPs^s (4Q98b)	DJD 16:154	Of no textual value.
Ps 6:2-4	11QPs^d (11Q8)	DJD 23:66	14 letters total; follows MT.
Ps 7:8-9	11QMelch (11Q13) 10-11	van der Woude, *OTS* 14:358	ע[ל]יה למרום שובה אל ידין עמים MT reads יהוה for לא.

Reference	Scroll	Location	Comments
Ps 7:14-31:22	5/6 ḤevPs (5-6 Ḥev1b)	Sanders, *JBL* 86:439.	Location of this text is difficult. Sanders (*JBL*) lists J. T. Milik in VTSup 9: 20, but this is an error for Milik, VTSup 4: 20. The text now appears in DJD 38:141-166.
Ps 9:3-6 (v. 4 N/R)	11QPsᵈ (11Q8)	DJD 23:66	Of no textual value.
Ps 9:3-8 (1 letter v. 8)	11QPsᶜ (11Q7)	DJD 23:54	Fragmentary; mostly follows MT; note that DJD lists as 9:3-7.
Ps 12:5-9 (3 letters v. 9)	11QPsᶜ (11Q7)	DJD 23:55	Very fragmentary; follows MT with some unique readings.
Ps 13:2-6 (v. 4 N/R)	11QPsᶜ (11Q7)	DJD 23:55	Very fragmentary; follows MT.
Ps 14:1-6 (3 letters v. 3; 2 letters v. 4; 3 letters v. 5)	11QPsᶜ (11Q7)	DJD 23:55	Fragmentary; follows MT except עולה for עלילה v. 1 (?).
Ps 15:1-5; 16 title	5/6 ḤevPs (5-6 Ḥev1b)	Yadin, *IEJ* 11:40	Identical to MT except omits לא רגל על לשנו in v. 3.
Ps 16:6-10	4QPsᶜ (4Q85)	DJD 16:51	Very fragmentary; follows MT; DJD omits reference to v. 6.
Ps 17:1(?)	4QPsᶜ (4Q85)	DJD 16:51	תפלה ל אזין
Ps 17:5-9	8QPs (8Q2)	DJD 3:148	Extremely fragmentary; follows MT.
Ps 17:9-15	11QPsᶜ (11Q7)	DJD 23:56	Fragmentary; several odd readings.
Ps 17:14	8QPs (8Q2)	DJD 3:148	יתרם Of no textual value.

Reference	*Scroll*	*Location*	*Comments*
Ps 18:1-12	11QPs^c (11Q7)	DJD 23:57	Fragmentary; follows MT except [תיכה]רחמ for ארחמך v. 2 (unique).
Ps 18:1-14 (2 letters v. 4; 3 letters v. 9; 4 letters v. 12; 3 letters v. 14)	4QPs^c (4Q85)	DJD 16:52	Extremely fragmentary; follows MT except ובינום v. 1.
Ps 18:6-9	8QPs (8Q2)	DJD 3:149	Extremely fragmentary; follows MT.
Ps 18:10-13	8QPs (8Q2)	DJD 3:149	Extremely fragmentary; follows MT.
Ps 18:15-17?	11QPs^c (11Q7)	DJD 23:59	Very fragmentary; identification questionable.
Ps 18:16-18 (2 letters v. 18)	4QPs^c (4Q85)	DJD 16:53	Very fragmentary; identical to MT.
Ps 18:26-29	11QPs^d (11Q8)	DJD 23:67	Fragmentary; follows MT; note that DJD has a misprint omitting עם before גבר v. 26, but the word is very clear on plate VII.
Ps 18:32-36	4QPs^c (4Q85)	DJD 16:53	No more than 3 letters per verse; of no textual value.
Ps 18:39-41	4QPs^c (4Q85)	DJD 16:53	Very fragmentary; identical to MT.
Ps 18:39-42 (v. 41 N/R)	11QPs^d (11Q8)	DJD 23:67	2-3 letters per verse preserved; mostly follows MT.
Ps 19:4-8 (1 letter v. 4; v. 6 N/R; 4 letters v. 7; 4 letters v. 8)	11QPs^c (11Q7)	DJD 23:59	Extremely fragmentary; textual value questionable.
Ps 21:10	4QNon-Canonical Pss B (4Q381)	DJD 11:105-106	Follows LXX in harmonizing to 2nd person.

Reference	Scroll	Location	Comments
Ps 22:14-17 (3 letters v. 14)	4QPs^f (4Q88)	DJD 16:88	Very fragmentary; several unique readings.
Ps 25:2-7 (v. 4 N/R; 3 letters v. 7)	11QPs^c (11Q7)	DJD 23:60	Very fragmentary; mostly follows MT.
Ps 25:8-12 (v. 9, 11 N/R)	4QPs^a (4Q83)	DJD 16:11	Very fragmentary; identical to MT.
Ps 25:15	4QPs^a (4Q83)	DJD 16:11	עִינִי תמיד
Ps 26:7-12	4QPs^r (4Q98a)	DJD 16:151	Very fragmentary; mostly follows MT.
Ps 27:1	4QPs^r (4Q98a)	DJD 16:151	ך יהוה אֹן
Ps 27:12-14	4QPs^c (4Q85)	DJD 16:54	Fragmentary; identical to MT.
Ps 28:1-5 (1 letter v. 3; 1 letter v. 5)	4QPs^c (4Q85)	DJD 16:54	Very fragmentary; identical to MT.
Ps 30:9-13	4QPs^r (4Q98a)	DJD 16:152	No more than 1 complete word per verse; mostly follows MT.
Ps 31:23-24 (1 letter v. 23)	4QPs^a (4Q83)	DJD 16:12	Very fragementary; follows MT.
Ps 31:24-25	4QPs^q (4Q98)	Milik, *Biblica* 38:245-255	One line with lacunae; follows MT.
Ps 33:1-12 (vv.1, 3, 7, 9 N/R; 3 letters v. 5; 3 letters v. 12)	4QPs^a (4Q83)	DJD 16:12	Immediately follows Ps 31; very fragmentary; otherwise follows MT.
Ps 33:1-18	4QPs^q (4Q98)	Milik, *Biblica* 38:245-255	Adds a title: לדוד שיר מזמור ; curious intrusion in v. 7; too broken up to reconstruct with accuracy; rest follows MT.
Ps 34:21-35:2 (1 letter 34:21; 35:1 N/R)	4QPs^a (4Q83)	DJD 16:12	Of no textual value.

Reference	Scroll	Location	Comments
Ps 35:4-20 (many vv. N/R)	4QPs^q (4Q98)	Milik, *Biblica* 38:245-255	Fragment of one column; follows MT.
Ps 35:13-20 (v. 19 N/R)	4QPs^a (4Q83)	DJD 16:13	Fragmentary; follows MT with some unique readings.
Ps 35:26-36:9 (35:28, 36:2, 4, 8 N/R)	4QPs^a (4Q83)	DJD 16:13	Very fragmentary; חפצי 35:27 (=LXX); other readings are unique.
Ps 35:27-28	4QPs^c (4Q85)	DJD 16:54	Fragmentary; identical to MT.
Ps 36:13-37:4 (1 letter 36:13; 2 or possibly 3 letters 37:4, see text)	11QPs^d (11Q8)	DJD 23:68	Extremely fragmentary; follows MT.
Ps 37:7-40	4QpPs^a (4Q171)	DJD 5:42-49	Includes pesher; mostly follows MT.
Ps 37:15	4QBarkhi Nafshi^d (4Q437)	DJD 29:311	Reverses תבוא and חרבם.
Ps 37:18-19	4QPs^c (4Q85)	DJD 16:55	Fragmentary; identical to MT.
Ps 38:2-12	4QPs^a (4Q83)	DJD 16:14	Fragmentary; mostly follows MT.
Ps 38:4-6 (v. 5 N/R)	4QXII^c (4Q78)	DJD 15:251	Recently re-identified as part of 4QPs^a (4Q83) but still listed in DJD 15 (see note there).
Ps 38:16-23	4QPs^a (4Q83)	DJD 16:15	Somewhat fragmentary; non-MT readings are unique.
Ps 39:13-40:1	11QPs^d (11Q8)	DJD 23:68-69	Extremely fragmentary; DJD lists through 40:2, but there are no discernible letters of v. 2; follows MT.
Ps 42:5	4QPs^c (4Q85)	DJD 16:55	המון חוגג
Ps 42:5	4QPs^u (4Q98d)	DJD 16:157	אלה רנה ותֿ

Reference	Scroll	Location	Comments
Ps 43:1-3 (1 letter v. 3)	11QPs^d (11Q8)	DJD 23:69	Extremely fragmentary; identical to MT.
Ps 44:3-5, 4, 7, 9, 23-24, 25	1QPs^c (1Q12)	DJD 1:72	Extremely fragmentary; follows MT.
Ps 44:8-9(?)	4QPs^c (4Q85)	DJD 16:55	ינו מ סל
Ps 45:1-2	4QpPs^a (4Q171)	DJD 5:45-50	Fragmentary; includes pesher; follows MT.
Ps 45:6-8 (1 letter v. 8)	11QPs^d (11Q8)	DJD 23:70	Adds אלף at end of v. 6 (?); otherwise follows MT.
Ps 45:8-11	4QPs^c (4Q85)	DJD 16:55	Fragmentary; follows MT.
Ps 47:2	4QPs^a (4Q83)	DJD 16:17	ים ם בקול
Ps 48:1-9 (vv. 4, 6, 8 N/R)	4QPs^j (4Q91)	DJD 16:118	Very fragmentary; follows MT except מלכ[י]ם v. 5 (=LXX^{mss}).
Ps 49:1-17 (2 letters v. 2)	4QPs^c (4Q85)	DJD 16:56	Follows MT except יבין v. 13 (−LXX).
Ps 49:6(?)	4QPs^j (4Q91)	DJD 16:119	רא בי
Ps 49:9-12	4QPs^j (4Q91)	DJD 16:119	Very fragmentary; follows MT except וחל[ן] for וחדל v. 9 (unique).
Ps 49:15	4QPs^j (4Q91)	DJD 16:119	לבלות
Ps 49:17	4QPs^j (4Q91)	DJD 16:119	איש כי
Ps 50:3-7 (vv. 4, 6 N/R)	11QPs^e? (11Q9)	DJD 23:77	Of no textual value.
Ps 50:14-23 (3 letters v. 15)	4QPs^c (4Q85)	DJD 16:57	Follows MT with a couple of spelling variations.
Ps 51:1-5	4QPs^c (4Q85)	DJD 16:57	Follows MT.
Ps 51:2-6 (2 letters v. 2)	4QPs^j (4Q91)	DJD 16:120	Very fragmentary; follows MT.

Reference	Scroll	Location	Comments
Ps 52:5-11 (1 letter v. 5; 3 letters v. 6)	4QPs^c (4Q85)	DJD 16:58	Mostly follows MT.
Ps 53:1	4QPs^c (4Q85)	DJD 16:58	Identical to MT.
Ps 53:2-54:6 (53:3, 6 N/R; 54:1, 4 N/R)	4QPs^a (4Q83)	DJD 16:17	Fragmentary; mostly follows MT.
Ps 56:4	4QPs^a (4Q83)	DJD 16:18	יום אירא
Ps 57:1, 4	1QpPs (1Q16)	DJD 1:81	Fragmentary; includes pesher; follows MT.
Ps 59:5-8 (v. 7 N/R)	11QPs^d (11Q8)	DJD 23:70-71	Very fragmentary; follows MT.
Ps 60:8-9	4QpPs^a (4Q171)	DJD 5:49-50	Fragmentary; includes pesher; follows MT.
Ps 62:13-63:4 (63:1, 3 N/R; 2 letters 62:13)	4QPs^a (4Q83)	DJD 16:18	Of no textual value.
Ps 66:16-67:8 (66:17 N/R; 3 letters 66:19; 67:3 N/R; 2 letters 67:7)	4QPs^a (4Q83)	DJD 16:19	Very fragmentary; a few unique readings.
Ps 68:1-5 (v. 2 N/R)	11QPs^d (11Q8)	DJD 23:71	Very fragmentary; identical to MT.
Ps 68:12-13, 26-27, 30-31	1QpPs (1Q16)	DJD 1:82	Very fragmentary; follows MT.
Ps 68:14-18 (1 letter v. 14)	11QPs^d (11Q8)	DJD 23:72	Very fragmentary; mostly follows MT.
Ps 69:1-19	4QPs^a (4Q83)	DJD 16:20	Appears to be rather poorly copied; virtually all readings are unique.

Reference	Scroll	Location	Comments
Ps 71:1-14	4QPsª (4Q83)	DJD 16:15	Immediately follows Ps 38; somewhat fragmentary; mostly follows MT.
Ps 76:10-12	4QPsᵉ (4Q87)	DJD 16:76	Very fragmentary; follows MT.
Ps 77:1	4QPsᵉ (4Q87)	DJD 16:76	לְאָס
Ps 77:18-78:1 (3 letters 77:18)	11QPsᵇ (11Q6)	DJD 23:40	Fragmentary; follows MT.
Ps 78:5-12 (2 letters v. 5)	11QPsᵈ (11Q8)	DJD 23:72-73	Fragmentary; follows MT.
Ps 78:6-7	4QPsᵉ (4Q87)	DJD 16:77	רון כסלם
Ps 78:31-33	4QPsᵉ (4Q87)	DJD 16:77	משמנ ולוא ה בבהל
Ps 78:36-37(?)	11QPsᵈ (11Q8)	DJD 23:75	יכזב ל
Ps 78:36-37 (?)	6QPs (6Q5)	DJD 3:112	בלשון מֶנ] [בב Of no textual value.
Ps 79:2-3	4QTanhumim (4Q176)	DJD 5:60-61	Semi-paraphrase with pesher; fragmentary.
Ps 81:2-3	4QPsᵉ (4Q87)	DJD 16:77	רנינו תוף
Ps 81:3-85:10	MasPsª (Mas1e)	Yadin, *IEJ* 15:104	Very fragmentary; according to Yadin, "the text corresponds to the MT in both the contents and the spelling" except that 83:7 reads אלהי for אהלי.

Reference	Scroll	Location	Comments
Ps 81:4-9 (3 letters v. 4; 1 letter v. 9)	11QPs^d (11Q8)	DJD 23:73	Fragmentary; mostly follows MT.
Ps 82:1	11QMelch (11Q13) 10	van der Woude, *OTS* 14:358	Follows MT except בקורב for בְּקֶרֶב.
Ps 82:2	11QMelch (11Q13) 11	van der Woude, *OTS* 14:358	Follows MT.
Ps 86:5-8 (v. 7 N/R)	1QPs^a (1Q10)	DJD 1:69	רְנִי טוב וסלח תפלתי והקש אִין Identical to MT.
Ps 86:10-11	4QPs^e (4Q87)	DJD 16:77	לבדך לִיך.
Ps 86:11-14	11QPs^d (11Q8)	DJD 23:74	Fragmentary; only variant of consequence is based on proposed reconstruction.
Ps 88:1-5 (2 non-contiguous letters v. 5)	4QPs^e (4Q87)	DJD 16:78	Very fragmentary; follows MT.
Ps 88:15-17 (3 letters v. 17)	4QPs^t (4Q98c)	DJD 16:155	Very fragmentary; אפורה for MT אפונה v. 16; otherwise follows MT.
Ps 89:20-31	4QPs89	Milik, *RB* 73:98-103	Many unique departures from MT.
Ps 89:44-48 (1 letter v. 48)	4QPs^e (4Q87)	DJD 16:78	Very fragmentary; follows MT except לְמִלְחמה for במלחמה v. 44 (unique).
Ps 89:50-53	4QPs^e (4Q87)	DJD 16:79	Very fragmentary; follows MT.
Ps 91:1-16 (v. 15 N/R)	11QApocryphal Pss (11Q11)	DJD 23:202-203 see also van der Ploeg, *RB* 72:210-217	Somewhat of a paraphrase with many additions, rearrangements, etc., but generally follows MT.

Reference	Scroll	Location	Comments
Ps 91:5-8, 12-15	4QPs^b (4Q84)	Skehan, *CBQ* 26: 313-322	Fragmentary; identical to MT.
Ps 92:4-8, 13-15	4QPs^b (4Q84)	Skehan, *CBQ* 26: 313-322	Fragmentary; generally follows MT.
Ps 92:12-14	1QPs^a (1Q10)	DJD 1:69	ים שמעה רז בלבנון יה שמעה is unique.
Ps 93:1-3	11QPs^a (11Q5) xxii	*DSPS* 76-77	Begins with Hallelujah; leans toward LXX.
Ps 93:3-5	4QPs^m (4Q94)	DJD 16:131	Very fragmentary; follows MT.
Ps 93:5	4QPs^b (4Q84)	Skehan, *CBQ* 26:313-322	ביתך נוה קדש [י]הוה לאר[ך] Follows MT.
Ps 94:1-9 (v. 5-6 N/R; 2 letters v. 4; 2 letters v. 7)	4QPs^b (4Q84)	Skehan, *CBQ* 26:313-322	Fragmentary; identical to MT.
Ps 94:10-18 (vv. 15-16 N/R)	4QPs^b (4Q84)	Skehan, *CBQ* 26:313-322	Very fragmentary; mostly follows MT.
Ps 94:16	1QPs^a (1Q10)	DJD 1:69	י יתיצב] [עלי א] [ן Of no textual value.
Ps 94:21-22	4QPs^b (4Q84)	Skehan, *CBQ* 26:313-322	Extremely fragmentary; of no textual value.
Ps 95:3-7 (2 letters v. 3; 3 letters v. 4)	4QPs^m (4Q94)	DJD 16:132	Very fragmentary; follows MT except ו[יבשה v. 5.
Ps 95:11-96:2	1QPs^a (1Q10)	DJD 1:69	אל מנוחתי ה שיר חדש ברכו שמו Identical to MT.
Ps 96:2	4QPs^b (4Q84)	DJD 16:33	ם ליו (see note on 98:4-5)

Reference	Scroll	Location	Comments
Ps 96:26; 98:4b	4QPs^b (4Q84)	Skehan, *CBQ* 26:313-322	[מיו]ם ליו[ם] ‏ [ור]נּנו וזמרו ‏ Identical to MT.
Ps 97:6-9 (4 letters v. 9)	4QPs^m (4Q94)	DJD 16:132	Fragmentary; follows MT (see note on 98:4-5).
Ps 98:4-5	4QPs^b (4Q84)	DJD 16:34	There seems to be a fair amount of confusion surrounding these particular fragments. See the Skehan entry under Ps 96:26; 98:4b and the DJD entry under Ps 96:2; Skehan appears to have identified the top line as 96:26 while DJD identifies it as 96:2. Textual value of this section of the MS is questionable.
Ps 98:4-8 (2 letters v. 8)	4QPs^m (4Q94)	DJD 16:133	Fragmentary; follows MT.
Ps 99:1	4QPs^v (4Q98e)	DJD 16:159	מֶלֶךְ יִרְגְּזוּ
Ps 99:1-5	4QPs^k (4Q92)	DJD 16:124	Identification questionable.
Ps 99:5-6	4QPs^b (4Q84)	Skehan, *CBQ* 26:313-322	[יהו]ה אלהינו ‏ ו להדם רגליו ‏ ש הוא ‏ הרן בכהניו ‏ Identical to MT.
Ps 100:1-2	4QPs^b (4Q84)	Skehan, *CBQ* 26:313-322	[ר] ‏ עבדו ‏ באו ‏ Of no textual value.
Ps 101:1-8	11QPs^a (11Q5) fragments A, B, C	*DSPS* 28-29	Very fragmentary; follows MT except יל for ילא in v. 2.
Ps 102: 1-2, 18-29	11QPs^a (11Q5) fragment C	*DSPS* 29-31	Fragmentary; mostly follows MT.

Reference	Scroll	Location	Comments
Ps 102:10-29 (3 letters v. 29)	4QPs^b (4Q84)	Skehan, *CBQ* 26:313-322	Somewhat fragmentary; mostly follows MT.
Ps 103:1	11QPs^a (11Q5) fragment C	*DSPS* 30-31	לדור רכי נפשי את ג Title obviously a visual error [לדוד for לדור]; of no textual value.
Ps 103:1-3	4QPs^b (4Q84)	DJD 16:39	Fragmentary; mostly follows MT; note that DJD does not list the unique reading עונך in v. 3.
Ps 103:2-11 (vv. 3, 5, 7 N/R)	2QPs (2Q14)	DJD 3:70	Fragmentary; follows MT.
Ps 103:4-11 (vv. 7-8 N/R)	4QPs^b (4Q84)	DJD 16:40-41	Follows MT.
Ps 103:12-14	4QPs^b (4Q84)	DJD 16:41	Follows MT.
Ps 103:20-21	4QPs^b (4Q84)	DJD 16:42	Non-MT readings may or may not be orthographic. Ps 112 follows.
Ps 104:1-3	4QPs^e (4Q87)	DJD 16:81	Fragmentary; may add לדויד as a superscription (=LXX); otherwise follows MT.
Ps 104:1-5	4QPs^d (4Q86)	DJD 16:67	Fragmentary; many unique readings, especially י for final ה.
Ps 104:1-6	11QPs^a (11Q5) fragment E	*DSPS* 160-161	Fragmentary; impossible to assign to one text.
Ps 104:3-5	4QPs^l (4Q93)	DJD 16:128	Non-MT readings are unique.
Ps 104: 6-11 (vv. 7, 10 N/R)	2QPs (2Q14)	DJD 3:71	Fragmentary; reads ולכו[ל מקום] in v. 8.
Ps 104:8-11	4QPs^d (4Q86)	DJD 16:69	Fragmentary; many unique readings.

Reference	Scroll	Location	Comments
Ps 104:11-12	4QPs¹ (4Q93)	DJD 16:129	Very fragmentary; identical to MT.
Ps 104:14-15	4QPsᵈ (4Q86)	DJD 16:69	Fragmentary; follows MT.
Ps 104:20-22	4QPsᵉ (4Q87)	DJD 16:81	Very fragmentary; follows MT.
Ps 104:21-35 (1 letter v. 21)	11QPsᵃ (11Q5) fragment E	*DSPS* 162-163	Fairly complete; readings lean toward LXX with several unique deviations; Ps 147 follows.
Ps 104:22-25	4QPsᵈ (4Q86)	DJD 16:70	Fragmentary; several unique readings.
Ps 104:33-35	4QPsᵈ (4Q86)	DJD 16:71	V. 34b is missing; adds כי before v. 35; otherwise follows MT.
Ps 105:1-3	4QPsᵉ (4Q87)	DJD 16:82	Extremely fragmentary; follows MT.
Ps 105:1-11	11QPsᵃ (11Q5) fragment E	*DSPS* 164-165	Fragmentary; several odd readings that destroy the sense of the text.
Ps 105:23-25 (1 letter v. 25)	4QPsᵉ (4Q87)	DJD 16:82	מצרים י מצריו ה
Ps 105:25-45	11QPsᵃ (11Q5) i	*DSPS* 34-35	Very fragmentary; generally follows MT.
Ps 105:36-45	4QPsᵉ (4Q87)	DJD 16:82	Very fragmentary; non-MT readings are unique.
Ps 106:48(?)	4QPsᵈ (4Q86)	DJD 16:66	Of no textual value; Ps 147 follows.
Ps 107:2-5 (1 letter v. 5)	4QPsᶠ (4Q88)	DJD 16:89	Very fragmentary; follows MT.
Ps 107:8-16 (3 letters v. 8)	4QPsᶠ (4Q88)	DJD 16:90	Very fragmentary; generally follows MT.
Ps 107:18-19	4QPsᶠ (4Q88)	DJD 16:91	Very fragmentary; follows MT.

Reference	Scroll	Location	Comments
Ps 107:22-30	4QPs^f (4Q88)	DJD 16:91-92	Very fragmentary; mostly follows MT except omits v. 30a.
Ps 107:26-27	4Q418b	DJD 34:498	Fragmentary; several unique readings.
Ps 107:35-42 (3 letters v. 38)	4QPs^f (4Q88)	DJD 16:93-94	Very fragmentary; poorly written; mostly follows MT.
Ps 108:8-9	4QpPs^a (4Q171)	DJD 5:49	Follows MT.
Ps 109:4-6	4QPs^f (4Q88)	DJD 16:95	Very fragmentary; all readings are unique.
Ps 109:13	4QPs^e (4Q87)	DJD 16:80	תּוֹ לְהַכְרִית
Ps 109:21-31 (v. 23 N/R)	11QPs^a (11Q5) fragment D	*DSPS* 32-33	Fragmentary; unique text.
Ps 109:24-28 (2 letters v. 24)	4QPs^f (4Q88)	DJD 16:96	Omits v. 26b; omits v. 27b; all other readings are unique; 3 apocryphal Pss follow.
Ps 112:1-9 (vv. 2, 4, 6, 8 N/R)	4QPs^w (4Q98f)	DJD 16:162	Very fragmentary; follows MT.
Ps 112:4-5	4QPs^b (4Q84)	Skehan, *CBQ* 26:313-322	Fragmentary; identical to MT.
Ps 113:1	4QPs^b (4Q84)	DJD 16:43	Of no textual value.
Ps 114:5	4QPs^e (4Q87)	DJD 16:80	חנוס
Ps 114:7	4QPs^o (4Q96)	DJD 16:140	ץְ וּמִלִּפְנֵי אֱלוֹהַּ יַעֲקֹ
Ps 115:1-2	4QPs^o (4Q96)	DJD 16:140	לָנוּ יהוה וְלוֹא וְאָמְרוּ הַגּוֹ
Ps 115:2-3	4QPs^b (4Q84)	Skehan, *CBQ* 26:313-322	Fragmentary; follows MT except omits נָא in v. 2.
Ps 115:4	4QPs^o (4Q96)	DJD 16:140	גּוֹיֵים

Reference	Scroll	Location	Comments
Ps 115:15-18	4QPsᵉ (4Q87)	DJD 16:80	Very fragmentary; mostly follows MT. Note that DJD lists a variant אדם for אדם v. 16 (typo?). The scroll reads אדם with MT, while a few MSS read האדם. Note also that the DJD variant listing is reversed, since the scroll actually agrees with the MT reading.
Ps 115:16-116:1	11QPsᵈ (11Q8)	DJD 23:75	No more than 4 letters per verse; of no textual value.
Ps 116:1-4 (2 uncertain letters v. 4)	4QPsᵉ (4Q87)	DJD 16:80	Very fragmentary; identical to MT.
Ps 116:3-5 (1 letter v. 3; v. 4 N/R)	4QPsᵒ (4Q96)	DJD 16:140	ו ואלוהינו מ
Ps 116:7-10	4QPsᵒ (4Q96)	DJD 16:140	May transpose last 2 phrases of v. 8; otherwise follows MT.
Ps 116:17-19	4QPsᵇ (4Q84)	Skehan, *CBQ* 26:313-322	Fragmentary; identical to MT.
Ps 118:1	11QPsᵇ (11Q6)	DJD 23:42	ם חסדו
Ps 118:1 (?), 15, 16, 8, 9, 29	11QPsᵃ (11Q5) xvi	*DSPS* 64-65	Strange conglomeration; several unknown additions.
Ps 118:1-3, 6-12, 18-20, 23-26	4QPsᵇ (4Q84)	Skehan, *CBQ* 26:313-322	Fragmentary; generally follows MT, but omits v. 11.
Ps 118:15-16 (2 letters v. 16)	11QPsᵇ (11Q6)	DJD 23:42	Extremely fragmentary; immediately follows v. 1; otherwise follows MT.
Ps 118:25-29	11QPsᵃ (11Q5), fragment E	*DSPS* 160-161	Fragmentary; follows MT.
Ps 118:26-27 (?)	4QPsᵇ (4Q84)	DJD 5:52-53	Includes pesher; of no textual value.

Reference	Scroll	Location	Comments
Ps 118:29	4QPs^e (4Q87)	DJD 16:81	טוב כי לע
Ps 119:1-6	11QPs^a (11Q5) vi	DSPS 44-45	Fragmentary; generally follows MT.
Ps 119:10-21	4QPs^h (4Q90)	RQ 64:16:483	Has some minority MT readings v. 17; otherwise follows MT.
Ps 119:15-28	11QPs^a (11Q5) vii	DSPS 46-47	Fairly complete; generally follows MT with some oddities of no textual import.
Ps 119:31-34, 43-48, 77-79	1QPs^a (1Q10)	DJD 1:69-70	Fragmentary; follows MT.
Ps 119:37-43	4QPs^g (4Q89)	RQ 64:16:479	Includes stanza division; most readings are unique.
Ps 119:37-49	11QPs^a (11Q5) viii	DSPS 48-49	Frequently deserts MT for its own tangents.
Ps 119:44-46	4QPs^g (4Q89)	RQ 64:16:480	Very fragmentary; follows MT.
Ps 119:49-50	4QPs^g (4Q89)	RQ 64:16:480	Very fragmentary; identical to MT.
Ps 119:59-73	11QPs^a (11Q5) ix	DSPS 50-51	Generally follows MT; adds אדוני (LXX) in v. 68.
Ps 119:73-74	4QPs^g (4Q89)	RQ 64:16:480	Very fragmentary; identical to MT.
Ps 119:81-83	4QPs^g (4Q89)	RQ 64·16:481	Very fragmentary; follows MT.
Ps 119:82-96	11QPs^a (11Q5) x	DSPS 52-53	Generally follows MT with the oddities normal to this scroll.
Ps 119:89-92 (1 letter v. 89)	4QPs^g (4Q89)	RQ 64:16:481	Very fragmentary; follows MT.

Reference	Scroll	Location	Comments
Ps 119:99-101, 104	5QPs (5Q5)	DJD 3:174	יְ תִי דְבְרֶךָ אֶרְחֹשָׂק Of no textual value.
Ps 119:105-120	11QPsᵃ (11Q5) xi	*DSPS* 54-55	Numerous readings, mostly unique.
Ps 119:113-120	5QPs (5Q5)	DJD 3:174	Extremely fragmentary; follows MT; some verses N/R?
Ps 119:128-142	11QPsᵃ (11Q5) xii	*DSPS* 56-57	Generally follows MT with the usual oddities characteristic of this scroll.
Ps 119:138-142	5QPs (5Q5)	DJD 3:174	Very fragmentary; follows MT.
Ps 119:150-164	11QPsᵃ (11Q5) xiii	*DSPS* 58-59	Generally follows MT with many unique readings.
Ps 119:163-165	11QPsᵇ (11Q6)	DJD 23:41	Very fragmentary; follows MT; note that DJD restores אה[ללכה v. 164 but does not explain the supplied *aleph*.
Ps 119:171-176	11QPsᵃ (11Q5) xiv	*DSPS* 60-61	Generally follows MT.
Ps 120:6-7	4QPsᵉ (4Q87)	DJD 16:83	בת שכנה לנפ
Ps 121:1-8	11QPsᵃ (11Q5) iii	*DSPS* 38-39	Text nearly complete; generally follows MT.
Ps 122:1-9	11QPsᵃ (11Q5) iii	*DSPS* 38-39	Fragmentary; mostly follows MT.
Ps 122:1-9	4Q522	DJD 25:68	Fragmentary; שם for MT שמה v. 5; [ש[ל[ו]ם] for MT שלוה v. 7; otherwise follows MT.
Ps 124:7-8	11QPsᵃ (11Q5) iv	*DSPS* 40-41	Fragmentary; mostly follows MT.

Reference	Scroll	Location	Comments
Ps 125:1-5	11QPsᵃ (11Q5) iv	*DSPS* 40-41	Generally follows MT.
Ps 125:2-5	4QPsᵉ (4Q87)	DJD 16:83	Fragmentary; a strange array of unique readings.
Ps 126:1-5	4QPsᵉ (4Q87)	DJD 16:83	Fragmentary; some apparent spelling errors.
Ps 126:1-6	11QPsᵃ (11Q5) iv	*DSPS* 40-41	Some unique ambiguities, but generally follows MT.
Ps 126:6	11QPsᵇ (11Q6)	DJD 1:71	נושאי אלום Of no textual value.
Ps 127:1	11QPsᵃ (11Q5) iv	*DSPS* 40-41	Fragmentary; follows MT.
Ps 127:1-5	1QPsᵇ (1Q11)	DJD 1:71	Fragmentary; follows MT.
Ps 127:2-3, 5	4QPsᵇ (4Q84)	DJD 5:51-52	Fragmentary; with pesher; follows MT.
Ps 128:3	1QPsᵇ (1Q11)	DJD 1:71	כנפן הפ כשתי Of no textual value.
Ps 128:3 6 (one letter v. 3)	11QPsᵃ (11Q5) v	*DSPS* 42-43	Fragmentary; אדוני for אֿ[ֿ]ֿ in v. 5.
Ps 129:1-8	11QPsᵃ (11Q5) v	*DSPS* 42-43	Generally follows MT.
Ps 129:7-8	4QPsᵇ (4Q84)	DJD 5:52	Follows MT. DJD lists one variant, but letter identification is questionable.
Ps 129:8	4QPsᵉ (4Q87)	DJD 16:84	אמר יהן
Ps 130:1-6 (v. 4, 5 N/R)	4QPsᵉ (4Q87)	DJD 16:84	No more than 2 letters per verse; of no textual value?
Ps 130:1-8	11QPsᵃ (11Q5) v	*DSPS* 42-43	Fragmentary; a few deviations but mostly follows MT.
Ps 131:1	11QPsᵃ (11Q5) v	*DSPS* 42-43	אֿ[ ]ל Of no textual value.

Reference	*Scroll*	*Location*	*Comments*
Ps 132:8-18	11QPsª (11Q5) vi	*DSPS* 44-45	Ps 119 follows in the column; mostly follows MT.
Ps 133:1-3	11QPsª (11Q5) xxiii	*DSPS* 78-79	Placed between Ps 141 and 144; text complete; mostly follows MT; adds שלום על ישראל at the end.
Ps 133:1-3	11QPsᵇ (11Q6)	van der Ploeg *RB* 74:411-412	Fragmentary; mostly follows MT; adds שלום ע]ל ישראל[at the end (cf. 11QPsª).
Ps 134:1-3	11QPsª (11Q5) xxviii	*DSPS* 88-89	Nearly complete; follows MT.
Ps 135:1-9 (v. 8 N/R; one letter v. 9)	11QPsª (11Q5) xiv	*DSPS* 60-61	Many unique deviations, otherwise follows MT.
Ps 135:6-8	4QPsⁿ (4Q95)	DJD 16:136	Unique addition to v. 6 (cf. 11QPsª); otherwise follow MT.
Ps 135:6-16 (2 letters v. 6; v. 9, 14 N/R; 2 letters v. 16)	4QPsᵏ (4Q92)	DJD 16:124	Extremely fragmentary; mostly follows MT.
Ps 135:11-12	4QPsⁿ (4Q95)	DJD 16:136	Includes a refrain כי לעולם חסדו; otherwise follows MT.
Ps 135:17-21	11QPsª (11Q5) xv	*DSPS* 62-63	Mostly follows MT.
Ps 136: 1-16	11QPsª (11Q5) xv	*DSPS* 62-63	Generally follows MT; one unique phrase in v. 7.
Ps 136:23-24 (3 letters v. 24)	4QPsⁿ (4Q95)	DJD 16:136	Follows MT except for position after Ps 135:12.
Ps 136:26b	11QPsª (11Q5) xvi	*DSPS* 64-65	Identical to MT.
Ps 137:1	11QPsª (11Q5) xx	*DSPS* 72-73	Follows MT.

Reference	Scroll	Location	Comments
Ps 137:9b	11QPsª (11Q5) xxi	*DSPS* 74-75	Follows MT.
Ps 138:1-8	11QPsª (11Q5) xxi	*DSPS* 74-75	Text complete; supports LXX addition of יהוה in v. 1; otherwise follows MT.
Ps 139:8-24	11QPsª (11Q5) xx	*DSPS* 72-73	Generally follows MT; supports MT over LXX in a few places, but does not do the reverse.
Ps 140:1-5	11QPsª (11Q5) xxvii	*DSPS* 86-87	Mostly follows MT.
Ps 141:5-10	11QPsª (11Q5) xxiii	*DSPS* 78-79	Generally follows MT.
Ps 141:10	11QPsᵇ (11Q6)	DJD 23:45	Of no textual value.
Ps 142:4-8	11QPsª (11Q5) xxv	*DSPS* 82-83	Follows MT except supports LXX in first clause of v. 5.
Ps 143:1-8	11QPsª (11Q5) xxv	*DSPS* 82-83	Follows MT with two unique readings.
Ps 143:2-4 (3 uncertain letters v. 2)	4QPsᵖ (4Q97)	DJD 16:143	Extremely fragmentary; follows MT.
Ps 143:6-8 (2 letters v 8)	4QPsᵖ (4Q97)	DJD 16:143	Extremely fragmentary; identical to MT.
Ps 144:1-2	11QPsᵇ (11Q6)	van der Ploeg *RB* 74:411-412	רי המלמ בי ומפל Of no textual value.
Ps 144:1-7	11QPsª (11Q5) xxiii	*DSPS* 78-79	Omits title; generally follows MT.
Ps 144:15	11QPsª (11Q5) xxiv	*DSPS* 80-81	Reads אשר for ש.

Reference	*Scroll*	*Location*	*Comments*
Ps 145:1-7	11QPsª (11Q5) xvi	*DSPS* 64-65	A few misspellings; adds a refrain, ברוך יהוה וברוך שמו לעולם ועד to each verse.
Ps 145:7-8	4Q521	DJD 25:10	Omits יהוה subject in each clause.
Ps 145:13-21	11QPsª (11Q5) xvii	*DSPS* 66-67	Many odd readings; adds a refrain, ברוך יהוה וברוך שמו לעולם ועד after each verse; textual value dubious.
Ps 146:9-10	11QPsª (11Q5) ii	*DSPS* 36-37	Adds an extra verse in between, origin uncertain. Otherwise follows MT.
Ps 147:1-2	11QPsª (11Q5) fragment E	*DSPS* 162-163	הלה בונה ירושלים Of no textual value except full spelling of "Jerusalem."
Ps 147:1-4	4QPsᵈ (4Q86)	DJD 16:66	Fragmentary; follows MT except possible dittography v. 1.
Ps 147:13-17 (4 letters v. 13, 4 letters v. 17)	4QPsᵈ (4Q86)	DJD 16:67	Fragmentary; follows MT except וחלב v. 14 (=LXX).
Ps 147:18-20	11QPsª (11Q5) fragment E	*DSPS* 164-165	Fragmentary; mostly follows MT.
Ps 147:20	4QPsᵈ (4Q86)	DJD 16:67	Fragmentary; follows MT.
Ps 148:1-12	11QPsª (11Q5) ii	*DSPS* 36-37	Omits initial הללו יה; otherwise follows MT.
Ps 149:7-9	11QPsª (11Q5) xxvi	*DSPS* 84-85	Unique addition before final יה הללו; otherwise follows MT.

Reference	Scroll	Location	Comments
Ps 150:1-6	11QPsᵃ (11Q5) xxvi	*DSPS* 84-85	Omits initial hallelujah; הנשמות for הנשמה in v. 6.
Ps 150:1-6	MasPsᵇ (Mas1f)	Y. Yadin, *Jerusalem Post* (Dec. 27, 1964)	Identical to MT.
Apocryphal Pss 151, 154, 155	11QPsᵃ (11Q5)	*DSPS*; cf. DJD 4:53-93	151 also found in LXX.
Prov 1:27-2:1	4QProvᵃ (4Q102)	DJD 16:182	Follows MT except מושכת for משובת 1:32.
Prov 7:9-11(?)	4QProvᵇ (4Q103)	DJD 16:186	ום ברת
Prov 13:6-9	4QProvᵇ (4Q103)	DJD 16:184	Very fragmentary; identical to MT.
Prov 14:5-10 (1 letter v. 5; vv. 6, 9 N/R)	4QProvᵇ (4Q103)	DJD 16:184	Very fragmentary; identical to MT.
Prov 14:12-13	4QProvᵇ (4Q103)	DJD 16:184	ואחרית תוגה
Prov 14:31-35	4QProvᵇ (4Q103)	DJD 16:185	Fragmentary; follows MT except may read וחסר v. 34 (=LXX).
Prov 15:1-8 (1 letter v. 6)	4QProvᵇ (4Q103)	DJD 16:185	Very fragmentary; identical to MT.
Prov 15:8	4Q271	DJD 18:181	Omits יהוה and thus reads תעובה for MT construct תועבת.

Reference	*Scroll*	*Location*	*Comments*
Prov 15:19-31	4QProv^b (4Q103)	DJD 16:186	Somewhat fragmentary; follows MT with 2 unique readings.
Eccl/ Qohelet 1:10-14	4QQoh^b (4Q110)	DJD 16:227	Very fragmentary; follows MT except אשר for ש v. 14; see DJD on possible inclusion of v. 15.
Eccl 5:13-17 (2 letters v. 13; 3 letters v. 16)	4QQoh^a (4Q109)	Muilenburg, *BASOR* 135: 22-28	Fragmentary; generally follows MT.
Eccl 6:1?	4QQoh^a (4Q109)	DJD 16:223	Of no textual value.
Eccl 6:3-8	4QQoh^a (4Q109)	Muilenburg, *BASOR* 135: 22-28	See also DJD 16:223; mostly follows MT; many unique readings; note comment about *BHS* footnote to v. 3.
Eccl 6:12	4QQoh^a (4Q109)	DJD 16:223	שָׁם יְגַ ש
Eccl 7:1-6	4QQoh^a (4Q109)	DJD 16:223	Fragmentary; many unique readings; otherwise follows MT.
Eccl 7:7-9 (DJD 16:225 lists vv. 7-10, but 1 letter v. 10)	4QQoh^a (4Q109)	Muilenburg, *BASOR* 135: 22-28	Fragmentary; generally follows MT.
Eccl 7:19-20	4QQoh^a (4Q109)	DJD 16:225	Extremely fragmentary; follows MT except 2 instances of ש for אשר.

Reference	Scroll	Location	Comments
Song 1:1-6, 6-7	6QCant (6Q6)	DJD 3:113	Fragmentary; generally follows MT.
Song 3:4-5	4QCantᵃ (4Q106)	DJD 16:199	אַ אָרְפֿנוּ עַד שֶׁ תָכֶם בְּנוֹתֽ Identification questionable; see DJD.
Song 3:7-11	4QCantᵃ (4Q106)	DJD 16:200	Very fragmentary; mostly follows MT except בנ[וֹת בנות ציון ירושלם for MT (LXX omits the phrase).
Song 2:9-17	4QCantᵇ (4Q107)	DJD 16:210	Fragmentary; profuse scribal errors; unexplained margin symbols.
Song 3:1-2	4QCantᵇ (4Q107)	DJD 16:210	Fragmentary; several scribal errors.
Song 3:5	4QCantᵇ (4Q107)	DJD 16:213	מָה רו
Song 3:7-8	4QCantᶜ (4Q108)	DJD 16.219	Very fragmentary; follows MT
Song 3:9-11 (1 letter v. 11)	4QCantᵇ (4Q107)	DJD 16:213	Very fragmentary; follows MT
Song 4:1	4QCantᵇ (4Q107)	DJD 16:213	עִיתֽי
Song 4:1-3	4QCantᵇ (4Q107)	DJD 16:214	Mostly follows MT.
Song 4:1-6	4QCantᵃ (4Q106)	DJD 16:200	Fragmentary; non-MT readings are unique.
Song 4:7	4QCantᵃ (4Q106)	DJD 16:202	Of no textual value.
Song 4:8-11	4QCantᵇ (4Q107)	DJD 16:214-215	Very badly written; profuse scribal errors.
Song 4:14-16	4QCantᵇ (4Q107)	DJD 16:217	Omits פרי v. 16; otherwise follows MT.
Song 5:1	4QCantᵇ (4Q107)	DJD 16:217	Fragmentary; follows MT.

Reference	Scroll	Location	Comments
Song 6:11-12	4QCant^a (4Q106)	DJD 16:202	פרחה מֶרְכָ
Song 7:1-7	4QCant^a (4Q106)	DJD 16:202	Extremely fragmentary; mostly follows MT.
Isa 1-66	1QIsa^a	Cross, *Scrolls from Qumran Cave I*; Burrows, *Dead Sea Scrolls of St. Mark's Monastery*, vol.1	Generally follows MT; see any of the many studies done on this scroll.
Isa 1:1 (?)	4QpIsa^e (4Q165)	DJD 5:28	ש י] הנ[ב][ואתן] וירושלם Presumably, the first word is a title.
Isa 1:1	3QpIsa (3Q4) (3Q4)	DJD 3:97	Fragmentary; a few LXX readings.
Isa 1:1-3	4QIsa^a (4Q55)	DJD 15:9	Fragmentary; identical to MT.
Isa 1:1-6	4QIsa^b (4Q56)	DJD 15:22	Fragmentary; follows MT.
Isa 1:1-6	4QIsa^j (4Q63)	DJD 15:23	Very fragmentary; וישראל v. 3 (=LXX).
Isa 1:4-14 (central vv. N/R)	MurIsa (Mur3)	DJD 2:80	Very fragmentary; identical to MT.
Isa 1:18-2:3	4QIsa^f (4Q60)	DJD 15:101-102	Numerous unique readings; otherwise follows MT.
Isa 1:10-16 (2 letters v. 10)	4QIsa^f (4Q60)	DJD 15:101	Very fragmentary; follows MT.

Reference	Scroll	Location	Comments
Isa 2:1-4	4QIsa^e (4Q59)	DJD 15:91	2 LXX readings, 2 1QIsa^a readings, but most readings follow MT.
Isa 2:3-16 (v. 5 N/R; v. 15 N/R)	4QIsa^b (4Q56)	DJD 15:23	Several odd spellings; otherwise follows MT.
Isa 2:7-10 (no certain letters v. 10)	4QIsa^a (4Q55)	DJD 15:10	Fragmentary; identical to MT.
Isa 2:22	1QS 5	Cross, *Scrolls from Qumran Cave I*	Follows MT.
Isa 3:14-22 (v. 19 N/R; v. 21 N/R)	4QIsa^b (4Q56)	DJD 15:24	Mostly follows MT; only LXX reading is questionable, see note p. 25 on line 8.
Isa 4:5-5:1 (1 letter 5:1)	4QIsa^a (4Q55)	DJD 15:10	Very fragmentary; ..לז for לילה 4:5 (unique?).
Isa 5:5-6	4QpIsa^b (4Q162)	DJD 5:15	[יץ גדרו ויהי למרמס יעלה שמיר Follows MT, except ויהי for והיה MT.
Isa 5:11-14	4QpIsa^b (4Q162)	DJD 5:15-16	Text complete; follows MT with some scribal errors.
Isa 5:13-14	4QIsa^f (4Q60)	DJD 15:103	לכן גל לכן
Isa 5:15-26 (4 uncertain letters v. 15)	4QIsa^b (4Q56)	DJD 15:25	Fragmentary; generally follows MT.
Isa 5:24-25	4QpIsa^b (4Q162)	DJD 5:16	Text nearly complete; follows MT.
Isa 5:25	4QIsa^f (4Q60)	DJD 15:103	תהיה ועודי

Reference	Scroll	Location	Comments
Isa 5:28-30	4QpapIsa^p (4Q69)	DJD 15:139	Very fragmentary; והבים for MT ונבט v. 30.
Isa 5:29-30	4QpIsa^b (4Q162)	DJD 5:16	ואין מ כנה מ בער Of no textual value.
Isa 6:3-8	4QIsa^f (4Q60)	DJD 15:103	Very fragmentary; ש[פתים v. 7 (unique); otherwise follows MT.
Isa 6:4-8 (3 uncertain letters v. 4; v. 7 N/R)	4QIsa^a (4Q55)	DJD 15:11	Very fragmentary; follows MT.
Isa 6:9 (?)	4QpIsa^b (4Q162)	DJD 5:17	ראור Of no textual value.
Isa 6:10-13	4QIsa^f (4Q60)	DJD 15:104	Very fragmentary; generally follows MT.
Isa 7:14-15	4QIsa^l (4Q65)	DJD 15:130	הנה חמאה
Isa 7:16-18	4QIsa^f (4Q60)	DJD 15:104	6 letters total; of no textual value.
Isa 7:17	4Q266	DJD 18:70	Restoration in DJD uncertain.
Isa 7:17	4Q267	DJD 18:109	Very fragmentary; appears to be a paraphrase.
Isa 7:17-20 (3 letters v. 17)	4QIsa^e (4Q59)	DJD 15:92	Very fragmentary; follows MT.
Isa 7:22-8:1	1QIsa^b (1Q8)	DJD 1:66	Fragmentary; follows MT.
Isa 7:23-8:1	4QIsa^f (4Q60)	DJD 15:104	Fragmentary; follows MT.
Isa 8:2-14 (3 letters v. 14)	4QIsa^e (4Q59)	DJD 15:92	Several unique readings; consistently spells עמנואל as one word; otherwise mostly follows MT.

Reference	Scroll	Location	Comments
Isa 8:4-11	4QIsa^f (4Q60)	DJD 15:105	Fragmentary; Syr word order v. 7; reading listed in v. 11 is speculative; otherwise follows MT.
Isa 8:7, 8, 9 (?)	4QpIsa^c (4Q163)	DJD 5:17	Fragmentary; mostly follows MT.
Isa 8:11	4QFlor (4Q174)	DJD 5:53	Fragmentary; follows MT.
Isa 8:11-14 (4 letters v. 14)	4QIsa^l (4Q65)	DJD 15:130	Very fragmentary; follows MT.
Isa 9:3-12 (1 letter v. 7; 4 letters v. 12)	4QIsa^c (4Q57)	DJD 15:50	Very fragmentary; mostly follows MT.
Isa 9:10-11	4QIsa^b (4Q56)	DJD 15:26	Extremely fragmentary; of no textual value.
Isa 9:11 (?), 14-20	4QpIsa^c (4Q163)	DJD 5:18	Very fragmentary; mostly follows MT.
Isa 9:17-10:10 (4 letters 10:9; 3 letters 10:10)	4QIsa^e (4Q59)	DJD 15:93-94	זרעיו 9:19 (spelling?); otherwise follows MT.
Isa 10:12, 13, 19 (?), 20-24	4QpIsa^c (4Q163)	DJD 5:18-19	Very fragmentary; follows MT.
Isa 10:17-19	1QIsa^b (1Q8)	DSSHU 45	Fragmentary; identical to MT.
Isa 10:21-34 (v. 23 N/R)	4QpIsa^a (4Q161)	DJD 5:11-13	Very fragmentary; no more than a few words per verse; follows MT.
Isa 10:23-33 (3 letters v. 26; 3 letters v. 30)	4QIsa^c (4Q57)	DJD 15:51	Several unique readings; אל for על v. 28 (=LXX); צבאות v. 33 is in paleo script.
Isa 11:1-5	4QpIsa^a (4Q161)	DJD 5:13-14	Very fragmentary; mostly follows MT.

Reference	*Scroll*	*Location*	*Comments*
Isa 11:4-11 (3 letters v. 11)	4QIsaᶜ (4Q57)	DJD 15:52	Several LXX readings; reading in v. 4 is questionable due to similarity of *waw* and *yod* (see plate VII).
Isa 11:7-9	4QIsaᵇ (4Q56)	DJD 15:26	Very fragmentary; identical to MT.
Isa 11:11-15	4QIsaª (4Q55)	DJD 15:11	Very fragmentary; ועפף for ועפו v. 14 (unique–scribal error?); otherwise follows MT.
Isa 11:14-15	4QIsaᵉ (4Q59)	DJD 15:94	ובזו א מצר
Isa 11:14-12:1 (2 letters 11:14)	4QIsaᶜ (4Q57)	DJD 15:53	Very fragmentary; follows MT.
Isa 12:1-13:4 (12:3 N/R; 12:5 N/R; 13:3 N/R)	4QIsaᵉ (4Q59)	DJD 15:95	Very fragmentary; ואמרת 12:4 (=LXX); otherwise follows MT.
Isa 12:2	4QIsaᵇ (4Q56)	DJD 15:27	אפחד
Isa 12:3-13:8 (12:5; 13:1,6 N/R)	1QIsaᵇ (1Q8)	DJD 1:66	Fragmentary; follows MT.
Isa 12:4-13:6 (12:6 N/R; 13:1 N/R; 13:15 N/R)	4QIsaª (4Q55)	DJD 15:12	Fragmentary; a fair number of unique readings.
Isa 12:5-13:6	4QIsaª (4Q55)	Muilenburg, *BASOR* 135: 28-32	Fragmentary; mostly follows MT.
Isa 13:3-18 (v. 12 N/R; 1 letter v. 15; 5 letters v. 18)	4QIsaᵇ (4Q56)	DJD 15:27	Fragmentary; follows MT with several spelling variations and 1 spelling error.
Isa 13:16-19	1QIsaᵇ (1Q8)	*DSSHU* 45	Fragmentary; follows MT.
Isa 14:1-5 (2 letters v. 5)	4QIsaᶜ (4Q57)	DJD 15:53	Very fragmentary; follows MT.

Reference	Scroll	Location	Comments
Isa 14:1-13 (1 letter v. 1; 2 letters v. 13)	4QIsaᵉ (4Q59)	DJD 15:95-96	Very fragmentary; numerous unique readings; omits כלם v. 10 (=Syr); otherwise follows MT.
Isa 14:8, 26-30	4QpIsaᶜ (4Q163)	DJD 5:19-20	Fragmentary; follows MT.
Isa 14:9	4QpIsaᵉ (4Q165)	DJD 5:29	בור כפגר Of no textual value.
Isa 14:13?	4QIsaᶜ (4Q57)	DJD 15:54	הר מן
Isa 14:20-24 (1 letter v. 20; 4 letters v. 21; 2 letters v. 22)	4QIsaᵉ (4Q59)	DJD 15:96	Extremely fragmentary; identical to MT.
Isa 14:28-15:2 (3 letters 14:28)	4QIsaᵒ (4Q68)	DJD 15:136	Fragmentary; very poorly written; mostly follows MT except for some scribal errors. Note use of final *mem* in all positions.
Isa 15:3-16:2	1QIsaᵇ (1Q8)	DJD 1:67	Fragmentary; follows MT.
Isa 15:4-6	4QpIsaᵉ (4Q165)	DJD 5:29	ריעו נ בכי יעלה ב ירק לו Follows MT.
Isa 16:7-11	1QIsaᵇ (1Q8)	*DSSHU* 45	Fragmentary; identical to MT.
Isa 17:8-18:1 (2 certain letters 18:1)	4QIsaᵇ (4Q56)	DJD 15:28	Fragmentary; mostly follows MT.
Isa 17:9-14	4QIsaᵃ (4Q55)	DJD 15:13	Fragmentary; identical to MT except 1 unique reading v. 11.
Isa 18:5-7	4QIsaᵇ (4Q56)	DJD 15:28	Fragmentary; several scribal oddities; generally follows MT.
Isa 19:1-25	4QIsaᵇ (4Q56)	DJD 15:28-30	Most non-MT readings are either unique or follow 1QIsaᵃ.

Reference	*Scroll*	*Location*	*Comments*
Isa 19:7-17	1QIsa^b (1Q8)	DJD 1:67	Fragmentary; follows MT.
Isa 19:9-12	4QpIsa^c (4Q163)	DJD 5:21	ואורגים שכר אגמֶ פרעוה ע אֲנִי בני מ Follows MT; uncertain in line 4 if אני or אנו is meant.
Isa 19:20-20:1	1QIsa^b (1Q8)	*DSSHU* 45	Fragmentary; identical to MT.
Isa 19:24-25	4QIsa^a (4Q55)	DJD 15:14	3 letters; of no textual value.
Isa 20:1-4 (4 letters v. 4)	4QIsa^b (4Q56)	DJD 15:30	Fragmentary; follows MT with 1 variant spelling of Isaiah's name.
Isa 20:2-6 (v. 5 N/R)	4QIsa^a (4Q55)	DJD 15:14	Very fragmentary; follows MT.
Isa 20:4-6 (3 letters v. 4)	4QIsa^f (4Q60)	DJD 15:106	Very fragmentary; follows MT.
Isa 21:1-16 (2 letters v. 2; no certain letters v. 3; v. 6 N/R; v. 11 N/R)	4QIsa^a (4Q55)	DJD 15:14	Very fragmentary; variants from MT are either unique or follow 1QIsa^a.
Isa 21:2 (?), 11-15	4QpIsa^e (4Q165)	DJD 5:29	Fragmentary; follows MT.
Isa 21:11-14	4QIsa^b (4Q56)	DJD 15:32	No more than 2 complete words per verse; identical to MT.
Isa 22:10-14 (2 letters v. 10)	4QIsa^c (4Q57)	DJD 15:54	Very fragmentary; follows MT with 1 spelling error.
Isa 22:11-18	1QIsa^b (1Q8)	DJD 1:67	Fragmentary; follows MT.
Isa 22:13d-23:6a	4QIsa^a (4Q55)	Muilenburg, *BASOR* 135: 28-32	Fragmentary; follows MT.

Reference	Scroll	Location	Comments
Isa 22:13-23:12	4QIsaᵃ (4Q55)	DJD 15:16	Fragmentary; variants from MT are either unique or follow 1QIsaᵃ.
Isa 22:14-22 (1 letter v. 14; 2 letters v. 22)	4QIsaᶠ (4Q60)	DJD 15:106	Very fragmentary; follows MT with numerous spelling variations and 1 error (יהסירך v. 19).
Isa 22:23	4QIsaᶜ (4Q57)	DJD 15:55	Of no textual value.
Isa 22:24-25	4QIsaᵇ (4Q56)	DJD 15:32	Very fragmentary; identical to MT.
Isa 22:24-23:4	1QIsaᵇ (1Q8)	*DSSHU* 45	Fragmentary; identical to MT.
Isa 22:25	4QIsaᶠ (4Q60)	DJD 15:107	Adds אדני before יהוה (=LXX).
Isa 23:8-18 (4 letters v. 8; 3 letters v. 9; v. 14 N/R)	4QIsaᶜ (4Q57)	DJD 15:55	Mostly follows MT with numerous scribal errors resulting in unique readings.
Isa 24:1-3	4QIsaᶠ (4Q60)	DJD 15:107	Very fragmentary; follows MT.
Isa 24:1-15	4QIsaᶜ (4Q57)	DJD 15:55-56	Numerous scribal errors and misspellings; some readings similar to LXX and Syr, but some may result from scribal errors.
Isa 24:2-4 (v. 3 N/R; 1 letter v. 4)	4QIsaᵇ (4Q56)	DJD 15:32	Identification uncertain.
Isa 24:18-25:8	1QIsaᵇ (1Q8)	DJD 1:68	Fragmentary; generally follows MT.
Isa 24:19-25:2 (4 letters 25:2)	4QIsaᶜ (4Q57)	DJD 15:58	Fragmentary; non-MT readings are unique.
Isa 25:8-12	4QIsaᶜ (4Q57)	DJD 15:59	Supports long LXX omission v. 9 (see *BHS* notes b, c-c); otherwise mostly follows MT.

Reference	*Scroll*	*Location*	*Comments*
Isa 26:1-5	1QIsa^b (1Q8)	*DSSHU* 46	Fragmentary; two unique readings.
Isa 26:1-7 (4 letters v. 1; v. 3 N/R; v. 6 N/R; 1 letter v. 7)	4QIsa^b (4Q56)	DJD 15:33	Extremely fragmentary; appears to read אדני for יהוה v. 4.
Isa 26:1-9	4QIsa^c (4Q57)	DJD 15:59	Fragmentary; non-MT readings are either unique or common to 1QIsa^a.
Isa 26:9-19 (v. 18 N/R; 4 letters v. 19)	4QIsa^b (4Q56)	DJD 15:33	Very fragmentary; several unique readings; otherwise follows MT.
Isa 27:1	4QIsa^f (4Q60)	DJD 15:107	Very fragmentary; identical to MT.
Isa 27:5-6 (1 letter v. 6)	4QIsa^f (4Q60)	DJD 15:108	Of no textual value.
Isa 27:8-10	4QIsa^f (4Q60)	DJD 15:108	Fragmentary; follows MT.
Isa 27:11-12	4QIsa^f (4Q60)	DJD 15:108	Very fragmentary; follows MT.
Isa 28:6-9 (3 letters v. 6; v. 8 N/R; 1 letter v. 9)	4QIsa^f (4Q60)	DJD 15:109	Of no textual value.
Isa 28:6-14 (2 letters v. 6; 3 letters v. 8; 2 letters v. 10)	4QIsa^c (4Q57)	DJD 15:60	Extremely fragmentary; follows MT.
Isa 28:15-19	1QIsa^b (1Q8)	*DSSHU* 46	Fragmentary; follows MT; reads with *Kethib* as opposed to *Qere* in v. 15.
Isa 28:16-17 (?)	4QIsa^f (4Q60)	DJD 15:109	Identification questionable; of no textual value.
Isa 28:18?	4QIsa^f (4Q60)	DJD 15:110	Of no textual value.
Isa 28:22	4QIsa^f (4Q60)	DJD 15:110	Of no textual value.

Reference	Scroll	Location	Comments
Isa 28:24?	4QIsa^f (4Q60)	DJD 15:110	יפתח
Isa 28:26-29:9 (4 letters 28:26; 29:5 N/R; 4 letters 29:9)	4QIsa^k (4Q64)	DJD 15:126	Very fragmentary; an inordinate number of spelling errors; very poorly written.
Isa 29:1-8	1QIsa^b (1Q8)	*DSSHU* 46	Average one word per verse extant; follows MT.
Isa 29:8?	4QIsa^f (4Q60)	DJD 15:110	Of no textual value.
Isa 29:10-11	4QpIsa^c (4Q163)	DJD 5:22	Fragmentary; supports *Kethib* over *Qere* in v. 11.
Isa 29:15-16	4QpIsa^c (4Q163)	DJD 5:22	ראנו ומי מעשה Of no textual value.
Isa 29:19-23	4QpIsa^c (4Q163)	DJD 5:22	Fragmentary; follows MT.
Isa 30:1-5	4QpIsa^c (4Q163)	DJD 5:23	Fragmentary; follows MT.
Isa 30:8-17 (4 letters v. 8; 2 letters v. 17)	4QIsa^c (4Q57)	DJD 15:61	Very fragmentary; כתו[ן] for MT כתבה v. 8; otherwise follows MT.
Isa 30:10-14	1QIsa^b (1Q8)	*DSSHU* plate 2	Very fragmentary; follows MT, except לפתח for MT לפתע in v. 13.
Isa 30:15-18	4QpIsa^c (4Q163)	DJD 5:24	Fairly complete; generally follows MT.
Isa 30:21-26	1QIsa^b (1Q8)	*DSSHU* plate 2	Very fragmentary; follows MT.
Isa 30:23	4QIsa^r (4Q69b)	DJD 15:143	ת האדמה ולחמ
Isa 31:1	4QpIsa^c (4Q163)	DJD 5:25-26	Fragmentary; follows MT except omits לעזרה .
Isa 31:8a	1QM (1Q33) 11:11-12	*DSSHU* plate 26	Follows MT.

Reference	Scroll	Location	Comments
Isa 32:5-6	4QpIsa^c (4Q163)	DJD 5:26	יקר נבלות עָה MT reads נבלה.
Isa 32:5-7	4QpIsa^e (4Q165)	DJD 5:29-30	Fragmentary; follows MT except omits יהוה after אל. There is a gap where the word would fit, why is uncertain.
Isa 33:2-8 (1 letter v. 3; 4 letters v. 7)	4QIsa^c (4Q57)	DJD 15:62	Very fragmentary; follows MT.
Isa 33:16-17(?)	4QIsa^a (4Q55)	DJD 15:18	Of no textual value.
Isa 33:16-23 (1 letter v. 16; 3 letters v. 17; 3 letters v. 18)	4QIsa^c (4Q57)	DJD 15:62	Very fragmentary; follows MT except may read ו[יהוה v. 22.
Isa 35:4-5	1QIsa^b (1Q8)	*DSSHU* plate 2	Fragmentary; follows MT.
Isa 35:9-36:2	4QIsa^b (4Q56)	DJD 15:34	Reads רבשקה as one word; otherwise follows MT.
Isa 37:8-12	1QIsa^b (1Q8)	*DSSHU* plate 2	Very fragmentary; follows MT.
Isa 37:29-32	4QIsa^b (4Q56)	DJD 15:34	Reads ו[אכול v. 30 (=*Kethib*) but omits פרים after it (unique).
Isa 38:12-39:8 (omits 38:13)	1QIsa^b (1Q8)	*DSSHU* plate 3	Generally follows MT with a few unique oddities.
Isa 39:1-8	4QIsa^b (4Q56)	DJD 15:35	Fragmentary; כי שמע for MT וישמע v. 1 (=LXX, 2 Kgs 20:12, see *BHS* note).
Isa 40:1-4 (3 letters v. 1; 3 certain letters v. 4)	4QIsa^b (4Q56)	DJD 15:35	Fragmentary; follows MT.

Reference	Scroll	Location	Comments
Isa 40:1-5	4QTanumim (4Q176)	DJD 5:60-61	Very fragmentary; numerous spelling errors; otherwise follows MT.
Isa 40:2-3	1QIsa^b (1Q8)	*DSSHU* plate 3	נרצה עונה יהוה ישרו א
Isa 40:3	1QS 8	Cross, *Scrolls from Qumran Cave I*	Begins at במדבר ; follows MT.
Isa 40:3	4QS^e (4Q259)	DJD 26:144	Editors suggest האמת to represent יהוה (the word is in a lacuna); otherwise follows MT.
Isa 40:12	4QpIsa^c (4Q165)	DJD 5:28-29	ושמים ב]ן [הָאָרֶץ שָׁקַל MT reads וׁשקל .
Isa 40:16, 18-19	5QIsa (5Q3)	DJD 3:173	אָ][אָ אֶל מִיתֹד בְ ירקע Identical to MT.
Isa 40:22-26	4QIsa^b (4Q56)	DJD 15:36	Scribal error תדרמינני v. 25, otherwise follows MT.
Isa 41:3-23 (v. 22 N/R)	1QIsa^b (1Q8)	*DSSHU* plate 4	Follows MT with two unique readings. Sukenik lists 41:7 as ולא , supporting LXX, but a lacuna here makes this questionable.
Isa 41:8-9	4QTanhumim (4Q176)	DJD 5:61	Very fragmentary; follows MT.
Isa 41:8-11	4QIsa^b (4Q56)	DJD 15:36	Very fragmentary; follows MT.
Isa 42:2-7	4QIsa^b (4Q56)	DJD 15:37	Very fragmentary; identical to MT.
Isa 42:4-11	4QIsa^h (4Q62)	DJD 15:118	Fragmentary; several scribal errors; mostly follows MT.

Reference	Scroll	Location	Comments
Isa 42:9-12	4QIsa^b (4Q56)	DJD 15:37	Very fragmentary; identical to MT.
Isa 42:14-43:4	4QIsa^g (4Q61)	DJD 15:114	Fragmentary; mostly follows MT.
Isa 43:1-2	4QTanhumim (4Q176)	DJD 5:62	וְיֹא אמר יה אָ כיא גאלתיך אתך אני וב]]ך Follows MT.
Isa 43:1-13, 23-27	1QIsa^b (1Q8)	*DSSHU* plate 5	Very fragmentary; follows MT.
Isa 43:4-6	4QTanhumim (4Q176)	DJD 5:62	Fragmentary; identical to MT.
Isa 43:12-15	4QIsa^b (4Q56)	DJD 15:37	Very fragmentary; follows MT.
Isa 43:16-24 (1 letter v. 16; 3 letters v. 17)	4QIsa^g (4Q61)	DJD 15:114	Very fragmentary; mostly follows MT.
Isa 44:3-7 (v. 4 N/R)	4QIsa^c (4Q57)	DJD 15:63	Very fragmentary; follows MT.
Isa 44:19-28	4QIsa^b (4Q56)	DJD 15:38	Fragmentary; mostly follows MT.
Isa 44:21-28	1QIsa^b (1Q8)	*DSSHU* plate 6	Fragmentary; follows MT.
Isa 44:23	4QIsa^c (4Q57)	DJD 15:63	ם פָּאר
Isa 45:1-4	4QIsa^c (4Q57)	DJD 15:64	Very fragmentary; follows MT.
Isa 45:1-13	1QIsa^b (1Q8)	*DSSHU* plate 6	Fragmentary; note v. 2 והרורים (MT והדורים, 1QIsa^a והררים with LXX).
Isa 45:6-8 (3 letters v. 6; 3 letters v. 7; 5 letters v. 8)	4QIsa^c (4Q57)	DJD 15:64	Follows MT.
Isa 45:20	4QIsa^d (4Q58)	DJD 15:77	הנשׂאֵי

Reference	Scroll	Location	Comments
Isa 45:20-46:3 (4 letters 45:24)	4QIsa^b (4Q56)	DJD 15:39	Fragmentary; follows MT.
Isa 46:3-13	1QIsa^b (1Q8)	DSSHU plate 7	Fragmentary; generally follows MT.
Isa 46:8-13 (4 letters v. 8)	4QIsa^c (4Q57)	DJD 15:65	Fragmentary; non-MT readings tend to be either unique or follow 1QIsa^a.
Isa 46:10-47:6	4QIsa^d (4Q58)	DJD 15:78	Fragmentary; a couple of unique readings; otherwise follows MT.
Isa 47:1-14	1QIsa^b (1Q8)	DSSHU plate 7	Fragmentary; follows MT.
Isa 47:8-9	4QIsa^d (4Q58)	DJD 15:79	Fragmentary; identical to MT.
Isa 48:6-8 (v. 7 N/R)	4QIsa^b (4Q56)	DJD 15:40	Extremely fragmentary; follows MT.
Isa 48:8-16 (4 letters v. 8)	4QIsa^d (4Q58)	DJD 15:79	Generally follows MT.
Isa 48:10-11 (4 letters v. 10; 5 letters v. 11)	4QIsa^c (4Q57)	DJD 15:65	איחל for MT יחל v. 11.
Isa 48:12-13	4QIsa^c (4Q57)	DJD 15:66	ראישון אליהם וי
Isa 48:14-15	4QIsa^c (4Q57)	DJD 15:66	אוהב יהו וא
Isa 48:17-19	4QIsa^c (4Q57)	DJD 15:66	Very fragmentary; mostly follows MT.
Isa 48:17-22	4QIsa^d (4Q58)	DJD 15:80	Fragmentary; follows MT.
Isa 48:17-22	1QIsa^b (1Q8)	DSSHU plate 8	Fragmentary; follows MT.
Isa 49:1-15	1QIsa^b (1Q8)	DSSHU plate 8	Fragmentary; generally follows MT.

Reference	*Scroll*	*Location*	*Comments*
Isa 49:1-15 (v. 3 N/R)	4QIsa^d (4Q58)	DJD 15:80	A few unusual readings; generally follows MT.
Isa 49:7, 13-17	4QTanhumim (4Q176)	DJD 5:61	Fragmentary; generally follows MT.
Isa 49:21-23 (4 letters v. 21)	4QIsa^b (4Q56)	DJD 15:40	Very fragmentary; identical to MT.
Isa 49:22	4QIsa^c (4Q57)	DJD 15:66	א כָתֶן תנ
Isa 50:7-11	1QIsa^b (1Q8)	*DSSHU* plate 9	Fragmentary; mostly follows MT.
Isa 51:1-2	4QIsa^b (4Q56)	DJD 15:40	Very fragmentary; identical to MT.
Isa 51:1-10	1QIsa^b (1Q8)	*DSSHU* plate 9	Fragmentary; follows MT.
Isa 51:8-16 (3 letters v. 8; 1 letter v. 10; 3 letters v. 14)	4QIsa^c (4Q57)	DJD 15:67	Extremely fragmentary; generally follows MT.
Isa 51:14-16 (v. 15 N/R)	4QIsa^b (4Q56)	DJD 15:40	Very fragmentary; identical to MT.
Isa 51:22-23	4QTanhumim (4Q176)	DJD 5:62	Fragmentary; quotation partly uncertain.
Isa 52:1-2	4QTanhumim (4Q176)	DJD 5:63	כי לוא] [ף יבוא פר ק] [מי Follows MT.
Isa 52:1-3	4QTanhumim (4Q176)	DJD 5:62-63	Fragmentary; follows MT.
Isa 52:2	4QIsa^b (4Q56)	DJD 15:41	מֵעפר קוּמִי
Isa 52:4-7	4QIsa^d (4Q58)	DJD 15:82	Very fragmentary; identical to MT.
Isa 52:7	11QMelch (11Q13) 15-16	van der Woude, *OTS* 14:358	Fragmentary; follows MT.

Reference	Scroll	Location	Comments
Isa 52:7	4QIsaᵇ (4Q56)	DJD 15:41	וה לציון
Isa 52:7-15	1QIsaᵇ (1Q8)	*DSSHU* plate 10	Fairly complete; mostly follows MT.
Isa 52:10-53:3 (2 letters 53:3)	4QIsaᶜ (4Q57)	DJD 15:68	Very fragmentary; follows MT except supralinearv א before זרוע 52:10 (unique).
Isa 53:1-12	1QIsaᵇ (1Q8)	*DSSHU* plate 10	Somewhat fragmentary; mostly spelling and scribal errors.
Isa 53:6-18 (3 letters v. 6)	4QIsaᶜ (4Q57)	DJD 15:69	Extremely fragmentary; identical to MT.
Isa 53:8-54:2	4QIsaᵈ (4Q58)	DJD 15:83	Several agreements with 1QIsaᵃ where it departs from MT.
Isa 53:11-12	4QIsaᵇ (4Q56)	DJD 15:41	Extremely fragmentary; identical to MT.
Isa 54:1-2	4Q265	DJD 35:62	Very fragmentary; follows MT.
Isa 54:1-6	1QIsaᵇ (1Q8)	*DSSHU* plate 10	Fragmentary; follows MT.
Isa 54:2-11	4QIsaᵈ (4Q58)	DJD 15:84	Very fragmentary; follows MT.
Isa 54:3-5	4QIsaᶜ (4Q57)	DJD 15:69	Extremely fragmentary; follows MT.
Isa 54:4-10	4QTanhumim (4Q176)	DJD 5.62-63	Fragmentary; follows MT.
Isa 54:7-8	4QIsaᶜ (4Q57)	DJD 15:69	Very fragmentary; ובחסדי for MT ובחסד v. 8 (=Syr).
Isa 54:9	4QIsaᶜ (4Q57)	DJD 15:69	נוח זאת
Isa 54:9-55:7 (1 letter 55:7)	4QIsaᶜ (4Q57)	DJD 15:70	Fragmentary; several unique readings and readings that follow 1QIsaᵃ.

Reference	*Scroll*	*Location*	*Comments*
Isa 54:10-13 (1 letter v. 10; 2 letters v. 13)	4QIsaq (4Q69a)	DJD 15:141	Extremely fragmentary; identical to MT.
Isa 54:11-12	4QpIsad (4Q164)	DJD 5:27-28	ויסדתיך בספי שמשותיך 90% pesher; of no textual value.
Isa 55:2-13	1QIsab (1Q8)	*DSSHU* plate 11	Generally follows MT.
Isa 56:1-12	1QIsab (1Q8)	*DSSHU* plate 11	Follows MT.
Isa 56:7-8	4QIsai (4Q62a)	DJD 15:121	Fragmentary; follows MT.
Isa 57:1-4	1QIsab (1Q8)	*DSSHU* plate 11	Generally follows MT.
Isa 57:5-8	4QIsai (4Q62a)	DJD 15:122	Fragmentary; identical to MT.
Isa 57:9-17	4QIsad (4Q58)	DJD 15:85	Fragmentary; only readings from MT are unique.
Isa 57:17-21	1QIsab (1Q8)	*DSSHU* plate 12	Follows MT.
Isa 57:18-58:3	4QIsad (4Q58)	DJD 15:86	Very fragmentary; mostly follows MT.
Isa 58:1-14	1QIsab (1Q8)	*DSSHU* plate 12	Text nearly complete; generally follows MT.
Isa 58:5-7	4QIsad (4Q58)	DJD 15:86	Very fragmentary; generally follows LXX.
Isa 58:13-14	4QIsan (4Q67)	DJD 15:133	Very fragmentary; an odd array of readings; very poorly written.
Isa 59:1-8	1QIsab (1Q8)	*DSSHU* plate 12	Fragmentary; mostly follows MT.

Reference	Scroll	Location	Comments
Isa 59:15-16	4QIsaᵉ (4Q59)	DJD 15:97	כאין משפט וירא כי אין נֶֽיִֽן
Isa 59:20-21	1QIsaᵇ (1Q8)	*DSSHU* plate 13	Only LXX reading occurs at a lacuna and so is debatable; follows MT.
Isa 60:1-22	1QIsaᵇ (1Q8)	*DSSHU* plate 13	Text nearly complete; mostly follows MT.
Isa 60:20-61:1	4QIsaᵐ (4Q66)	DJD 15:132	Very fragmentary; follows MT.
Isa 61:1	11QMelch (11Q13) 6	van der Woude, *OTS* 14:358	וקרא להמה דרר Identification questionable; MT reads לקרא לשבוים דרור.
Isa 61:1-2	1QIsaᵇ (1Q8)	*DSSHU* plate 13	Fragmentary; follows MT.
Isa 61:1-3	4QIsaᵇ (4Q56)	DJD 15:42	Very fragmentary; identical to MT.
Isa 62:2-12	1QIsaᵇ (1Q8)	*DSSHU* plate 14	Fairly complete; mostly follows MT.
Isa 63:1-19	1QIsaᵇ (1Q8)	*DSSHU* plate 14	Fairly complete; mostly follows MT.
Isa 64:1, 6-8	1QIsaᵇ (1Q8)	*DSSHU* plate 14	Very fragmentary; follows MT.
Isa 64:5-65.1	4QIsaᵇ (4Q56)	DJD 15:42	Very fragmentary; mostly follows MT.
Isa 65:17-25	1QIsaᵇ (1Q8)	*DSSHU* plate 15	Somewhat fragmentary; follows MT.
Isa 66:1-24	1QIsaᵇ (1Q8)	*DSSHU* plate 15	Fragmentary; follows MT.
Isa 66:20-24	4QIsaᶜ (4Q57)	DJD 15:71	Very fragmentary; follows MT except בשבתה v. 23 (cf *BHS* note).

Reference	*Scroll*	*Location*	*Comments*
Isa 66:24	4QIsa[b] (4Q56)	DJD 15:42	Very fragmentary; identical to MT.

Reference	*Scroll*	*Location*	*Comments*
Jer 4:5	4QJer[c] (4Q72)	DJD 15:184	המבצר
Jer 4:13-16	4QJer[c] (4Q72)	DJD 15:185	Very fragmentary; identical to MT.
Jer 7:1-2	4QJer[a] (4Q70)	DJD 15:154	ר עמד
Jer 7:15-19 (4 letters v. 15; 2 letters v. 17; 2 letters v. 19)	4QJer[a] (4Q70)	DJD 15:154	Extremely fragmentary; identical to MT.
Jer 7:28-8:12 (8:4 N/R)	4QJer[a] (4Q70)	DJD 15:155	Very fragmentary; mostly follows MT.
Jer 7:29-9:2 (8:8-22 N/R)	4QJer[a] (4Q70)	Janzen, *Studies in the Text of Jer* 174	Fragmentary; mostly follows MT.
Jer 8:1-3 (2 letters v. 1)	4QJer[c] (4Q72)	DJD 15:185	Fragmentary; mostly follows MT.
Jer 8:19-9:2 (8:20-22 N/R)	4QJer[a] (4Q70)	DJD 15:155	Very fragmentary; follows MT.
Jer 8:21-9:5 (3 letters 9:4; 3 letters 9:5)	4QJer[c] (4Q72)	DJD 15:186	Fragmentary; adds צְבָ[אות] above the line at the end of 9:2; otherwise follows MT.
Jer 9:7-14	4QJer[a] (4Q70)	Janzen, *Studies* 175	Somewhat fragmentary; follows MT.
Jer 9:7-15	4QJer[a] (4Q70)	DJD 15:157	Very fragmentary; mostly follows MT.

Reference	Scroll	Location	Comments
Jer 9:22-10:21 (9:24 N/R; 10:1 N/R; 10:5a,b N/R; 10:12, 14, 17, 19 N/R)	4QJer^b (4Q71)	DJD 15:173 see also Janzen, *Studies* 181-182	Very fragmentary; follows LXX in omission of 10:6-8 and order of 10:5a, 9, 5b; includes some unique readings and several MT readings.
Jer 10:9-14 (4 letters v. 9)	4QJer^a (4Q70)	DJD 15:158 see also Janzen, *Studies* 175	Very fragmentary; follows MT.
Jer 10:12-13	4QJer^c (4Q72)	DJD 15:187	Very fragmentary; identical to MT.
Jer 10:23	4QJer^a (4Q70)	DJD 15:159	הלך הכין אֹ
Jer 11:3-6	4QJer^a (4Q70)	DJD 15:159 see also Janzen, *Studies* 176	Very fragmentary; follows MT.
Jer 11:19-20	4QJer^a (4Q70)	DJD 15:159	Very fragmentary; follows MT except יוזכר עד for MT יזכר עוד v. 19 (unique).
Jer 12:3-7 (4 letters v. 3; 4 letters v. 7)	4QJer^a (4Q70)	DJD 15:160 see also Janzen, *Studies* 176	Janzen lists as 12:3-6, very fragmentary; adds יראנכמה יה[וה] after v. 4 (=LXX?).
Jer 12:13-16 (4 letters v. 15)	4QJer^a (4Q70)	DJD 15:160 see also Janzen, *Studies* 177	Very fragmentary; follows MT except נתושם v. 14 (spelling?).
Jer 12:17-13:7 (3 letters 13:7)	4QJer^a (4Q70)	DJD 15:161 see also Janzen, *Studies* 177	Fragmentary; mostly follows MT.
Jer 13:22 (?)	2QJer (2Q13)	DJD 3:69	תְאָ עֲק Of no textual value.
Jer 13:22?	4QJer^a (4Q70)	DJD 15:161	חמס תְ

Reference	Scroll	Location	Comments
Jer 13:27	4QJer^a (4Q70)	DJD 15:162	אֵ תמהר י אֵ
Jer 14:4-7	4QJer^a (4Q70)	DJD 15:162 see also Janzen, *Studies* 178	Fragmentary; follows MT with some spelling errors.
Jer 15:1-2	4QJer^a (4Q70)	Janzen, *Studies* 178 see also DJD 15:162	מצל פני וה ר למות Follows MT.
Jer 17:8-26 (4 letters v. 9)	4QJer^a (4Q70)	DJD 15:163 see also Janzen, *Studies* 178-179	Fragmentary; generally follows MT but very poorly written.
Jer 18:15-19:1 (3 letters 19:1)	4QJer^a (4Q70)	DJD 15:165 see also Janzen, *Studies* 179-180	Fragmentary; mostly follows MT.
Jer 19:8-9	4QJer^c (4Q72)	DJD 15:187	לכ עובר אָכְלו בשר Line 2 appears to follow LXX.
Jer 20:2-5	4QJer^c (4Q72)	DJD 15:187	Very fragmentary; mostly follows MT.
Jer 20:7-9 (1 letter v. 9)	4QJer^c (4Q72)	DJD 15:188	Very fragmentary; identical to MT.
Jer 20:13-15	4QJer^c (4Q72)	DJD 15:188	ל לדתי לאמ
Jer 20:14-21:1 (4 letters 20:14; 2 letters 20:17; 1 letter 20:18; 4 letters 21:1)	4QJer^a (4Q70)	DJD 15:167	Extremely fragmentary; follows MT.
Jer 21:7-10 (3 letters v. 10)	4QJer^c (4Q72)	DJD 15:189	Very fragmentary; only suggested LXX reading is reconstructed; most other readings are unique.

Reference	Scroll	Location	Comments
Jer 22:4-6	4QJer^c (4Q72)	DJD 15:189	Very fragmentary; follows MT including *Qere* reading v. 4.
Jer 22:3-16 (4 letters v. 3)	4QJer^a (4Q70)	DJD 15:167-168 see also Janzen, *Studies* 180-181	Janzen lists as 22:4-16; fragmentary; generally follows MT though poorly written with many spelling oddities.
Jer 22:10-17	4QJer^c (4Q72)	DJD 15:190	Very fragmentary; several unique readings.
Jer 22:17-28	4QJer^c (4Q72)	DJD 15:191	Fragmentary; non-MT readings are unique.
Jer 25:7-8	4QJer^c (4Q72)	DJD 15:192	Very fragmentary; identical to MT.
Jer 25:15-17	4QJer^c (4Q72)	DJD 15:193	Fragmentary; follows MT except אני for אנכי v. 16.
Jer 25:24-26	4QJer^c (4Q72)	DJD 15:193	Very fragmentary; follows MT.
Jer 26:10?	4QJer^a (4Q70)	DJD 15:169	יהודה את
Jer 26:10-13	4QJer^c (4Q72)	DJD 15:194	Very fragmentary; follows MT.
Jer 27:1-3 (3 letters v. 1)	4QJer^c (4Q72)	DJD 15:194	Very fragmentary; mostly follows MT.
Jer 27:13-15 (3 letters v. 13; 3 letters v. 15)	4QJer^c (4Q72)	DJD 15:194	Very fragmentary; identical to MT.
Jer 30:6-9	4QJer^c (4Q72)	DJD 15:195	Very fragmentary; follows MT.
Jer 30:17-31:4	4QJer^c (4Q72)	DJD 15:196	Fragmentary; generally follows MT.
Jer 31:4-14 (v. 10 N/R; 2 letters v. 11)	4QJer^c (4Q72)	DJD 15:197-198	Fragmentary; a few LXX readings but generally follows MT.

Reference	Scroll	Location	Comments
Jer 31:19-26 (3 letters v. 20; 3 letters v. 23; v. 24 N/R; 4 letters v. 25)	4QJerᶜ (4Q72)	DJD 15:199	Very fragmentary; follows MT.
Jer 32:24-25 (?)	2QJer (2Q13)	DJD 3:69	וְאֲשֶׁר לכה Of no textual value.
Jer 33:16-20	4QJerᶜ (4Q72)	DJD 15:200	Very fragmentary; follows MT.
Jer 42:7-11, 14	2QJer (2Q13)	DJD 3:63	Very fragmentary; generally follows MT.
Jer 43:2-10 (1 letter v. 2; 1 letter v. 10)	4QJerᵈ (4Q72a)	DJD 15:203	Very fragmentary; mostly follows LXX.
Jer 43:3-9	4QJerᵇ (4Q71)	Janzen, *Studies* 182-183	Fairly complete; leans significantly (according to Janzen) toward LXX tradition.
Jer 43:8-11	2QJer (2Q13)	DJD 3:63-64	Very fragmentary; follows MT.
Jer 44:1-3	2QJer (2Q13)	DJD 3:64	Fragmentary; follows MT.
Jer 44:12-14	2QJer (2Q13)	DJD 3:64	עב פקד ב ובר יִהְוּ Follows MT except for ובר[עב] (LXX).
Jer 46:27-47:7	2QJer (2Q13)	DJD 3:65	Very fragmentary; generally follows MT.
Jer 48:2-4 (?)	2QJer (2Q13)	DJD 3:69	חֶרֶב קוֹל קֶה צְעָוֹרִיה Of no textual value.
Jer 48:7	2QJer (2Q13)	DJD 3:66	אתה Of no textual value.

Reference	Scroll	Location	Comments
Jer 48:25-39	2QJer (2Q13)	DJD 3:66	Very fragmentary; generally follows MT.
Jer 48:41-42 (?)	2QJer (2Q13)	DJD 3:69	גבו על יהוה Of no textual value.
Jer 48:43-45	2QJer (2Q13)	DJD 3:68	ה עולה הוה מקרית Follows MT.
Jer 50:4-6	4QJer^b (4Q71)	Janzen, *Studies* 184	Fragmentary; follows MT.
Jer 50:4-6	4QJer^e (4Q72b)	DJD 15:207	Very fragmentary; follows MT.

Reference	Scroll	Location	Comments
Lam 1 and 4	4QapLam (4Q179)	DJD 5:75-77	Mostly one- or two-word allusions to Lamentations. Nothing solid.
Lam 1:1-6	4QLam (4Q111)	DJD 16:231	Very fragmentary; follows MT.
Lam 1:6-10 (1 letter v. 10)	4QLam (4Q111)	DJD 16:232	Very poorly written (see DJD intro); profusion of unique and clearly erroneous readings makes textual value questionable.
Lam 1:10-12	3QLam (3Q3)	DJD 3:95	קהל גֿוֿגֿٍ הוֹגֿ Of no textual value.
Lam 1:10-15, 17, 16, 18	4QLam (4Q111)	DJD 16:234	"The text is in considerable disorder," p.234, footnote to 1:10-11.

Reference	*Scroll*	*Location*	*Comments*
Lam 3:53, 56, 59, 62	3QLam (3Q3)	DJD 3:95	צמתו ב קולי שמע ראי שֶׁ] [חָ Of no textual value.
Lam 4:5-8, 11-15, 15-16, 19-20	5QLamᵃ (5Q6)	DJD 3:176	Very fragmentary; several unique readings.
Lam 4:17-20	5QLamᵇ (5Q7)	DJD 3:178	יְנה צדו צעָ קלים הְ אפינו Of no textual value.
Lam 4:20-5:3, 4-12, 12-13, 16-17	5QLamᵃ (5Q6)	DJD 3:176-177	Very fragmentary; generally follows MT.

Ezek 1:8-10 (2 letters v. 10)	11QEzek (11Q4)	DJD 23:22	Very fragmentary; identical to MT; note that DJD restores בלכ]תם v. 9 rather than MT בלכתן.
Ezek 1:10-13	4QEzekᵇ (4Q74)	DJD 15:216-217	Somewhat fragmentary; generally follows MT.
Ezek 1:16-19 (v. 18 N/R; 1 letter v. 19)	4QEzekᵇ (4Q74)	DJD 15:217	Of no textual value.
Ezek 1:20-24	4QEzekᵇ (4Q74)	DJD 15:218	Mostly follows MT.
Ezek 4:3-5 (4 letters v. 5)	11QEzek (11Q4)	DJD 23:23	Very fragmentary; identical to MT.
Ezek 4:5-6(?)	11QUnclassified Fragments (11Q30)	DJD 23:442	למספר יְ דְ ה

Reference	Scroll	Location	Comments
Ezek 4:6	11QEzek (11Q4)	DJD 23:24	Very fragmentary; identical to MT.
Ezek 4:9-10 (2 letters v. 9)	11QEzek (11Q4)	DJD 23:24	Very fragmentary; identical to MT.
Ezek 4:16-5:1	1QEzek (1Q9)	DJD 1:69	Very fragmentary; follows MT.
Ezek 5:11-17	11QEzek (11Q4)	Brownlee, *RevQ* 4:14 and DJD 23:24-25	Very fragmentary; mostly follows MT (see DJD discussion vs. Brownlee on 5:15).
Ezek 7:9-12 (v. 10 N/R; 2 letters v. 12)	11QEzek (11Q4)	Brownlee, *RevQ* 4:16 and DJD 23:27	חוס עי יהוה מכה למטה רשע לא מ שמ Follows MT.
Ezek 10:6-16 (3 letters v. 16)	4QEzek^a (4Q73)	DJD 15:211	Fragmentary; ידי v. 8 (=LXX); otherwise follows MT.
Ezek 10:11	11QEzek (11Q4)	Brownlee, *RevQ* 4:16	בית סבו בלכ Of no textual value.
Ezek 10:17-11.11 (11:4 N/R; 2 letters 11:11)	4QEzck^a (4Q73)	DJD 15:212	Fragmentary; mostly follows MT.
Ezek 16:31-33 (v. 32 N/R)	3QEzek (3Q1)	DJD 3:94	נ[ ]ת[ ]גב נה לקלס ל Follows MT.
Ezek 23:14-18 (v. 16 N/R)	4QEzek^a (4Q73)	DJD 15:213	No more than 5 letters per verse; of no textual value.
Ezek 23:44-47	4QEzek^a (4Q73)	DJD 15:213	Some apparent spelling errors; ויבאו v. 44 (=some MT mss, LXX).

Reference	*Scroll*	*Location*	*Comments*
Ezek 24:2-3	4QEzek^c (4Q75)	DJD 15:219	Very fragmentary; identical to MT.
Ezek 37:23 (?)	4QFlor (4Q174)	DJD 5:53	לו ליהמה [ ] ל
Ezek 41:3-6 (2 letters v. 6)	4QEzek^a (4Q73)	DJD 15:214	Fragmentary; omits final סביב v. 5.

Dan 1:10-17	1QDan^a (1Q71)	DJD 1:150	Fragmentary; follows MT except זרעים for זרענים in v. 16.
Dan 1:16-20	4QDan^a (4Q112)	Ulrich, *BASOR* 268: 17-37	Very fragmentary; readings uncertain.
Dan 2:2-6	1QDan^a (1Q71)	DJD 1:150	Fragmentary; mostly follows MT.
Dan 2:9-11	4QDan^a (4Q112)	Ulrich, *BASOR* 268: 17-37	Extremely fragmentary; of no textual value.
Dan 2:19-33	4QDan^a (4Q112)	Ulrich, *BASOR* 268:17-37	A wide range of readings, most unique.
Dan 2:33-46	4QDan^a (4Q112)	Ulrich, *BASOR* 268: 17-37	Fragmentary; most readings unique.
Dan 2:47-3:2	4QDan^a (4Q112)	Ulrich, *BASOR* 268:17-37	Very fragmentary; follows MT with one spelling error (proper name).
Dan 3:8-10?	4QDan^d (4Q115)	DJD 16:280	Of no textual value.
Dan 3:22-28	1QDan^b (1Q72)	DJD 1:151	Fragmentary; follows MT.
Dan 3:23-25	4QDan^d (4Q115)	DJD 16:281	Fragmentary; mostly follows MT.
Dan 3:27-30	1QDan^b (1Q72)	DJD 1:151-152	Fragmentary; mostly follows MT.

Reference	Scroll	Location	Comments
Dan 4:5-9 (1 letter v. 7)	4QDan^d (4Q115)	DJD 16:282	Extremely fragmentary; mostly follows MT.
Dan 4:12-16	4QDan^d (4Q115)	DJD 16:283	Very fragmentary; generally follows MT.
Dan 4:29-30	4QDan^a (4Q112)	Ulrich, *BASOR* 268: 17-37	Only four complete letters; of no textual value.
Dan 5:5-7	4QDan^a (4Q112)	Ulrich, *BASOR* 268: 17-37	Very fragmentary; frequently writes א for MT ה.
Dan 5:10-16	4QDan^b (4Q113)	Ulrich, *BASOR* 274: 3-26	Extremely fragmentary; follows MT with one conjectured variant.
Dan 5:12-13	4QDan^a (4Q112)	Ulrich, *BASOR* 268: 17-37	Very fragmentary; generally follows MT.
Dan 5:13-14	4QDan^a (4Q112)	Ulrich, *BASOR* 268: 17-37	Extremely fragmentary; identical to MT.
Dan 5:16-19	4QDan^a (4Q112)	Ulrich, *BASOR* 268: 17-37	Very little of v. 19; follows MT with two spelling variations
Dan 5:19-22	4QDan^b (4Q113)	Ulrich, *BASOR* 274: 3-26	Extremely fragmentary; follows MT.
Dan 6:8-13	4QDan^b (4Q113)	Ulrich, *BASOR* 274: 3-26	Very fragmentary; follows MT.
Dan 6:13-22 (2 letters v. 22)	4QDan^b (4Q113)	Ulrich, *BASOR* 274: 3-26	Fragmentary; mostly follows MT.
Dan 6:27-7:4	4QDan^b (4Q113)	Ulrich, *BASOR* 274: 3-26	Extremely fragmentary; follows MT.
Dan 7:5-6 (?)	4QDan^b (4Q113)	Ulrich, *BASOR* 274: 3-26	Of no textual value.
Dan 7:5-7	4QDan^a (4Q112)	Ulrich, *BASOR* 268: 17-37	Extremely fragmentary; mostly follows MT.
Dan 7:15-23 (1 letter v. 20)	4QDan^d (4Q115)	DJD 16:284	Fragmentary; identical to MT.

Reference	*Scroll*	*Location*	*Comments*
Dan 7:25-8:5	4QDanª (4Q112)	Ulrich, *BASOR* 268: 17-37	Mostly follows MT with some unique readings.
Dan 7:26-28 (1 letter v. 26)	4QDanᵇ (4Q113)	Ulrich, *BASOR* 274: 3-26	Extremely fragmentary; follows MT.
Dan 8:1-8	4QDanᵇ (4Q113)	Ulrich, *BASOR* 274: 3-26	Fragmentary; mostly follows MT.
Dan 8:13-16	4QDanᵇ (4Q113)	Ulrich, *BASOR* 274: 3-26	Fragmentary; follows MT.
Dan 8:16-17 (?)	6QDan (6Q7)	DJD 3:116	הֻמַר הָב Of no textual value.
Dan 8:20-21 (?)	6QDan (6Q7)	DJD 3:114	רא מלך יון ל
Dan 9:12-14	4QDanᵉ (4Q116)	DJD 16:288	Very fragmentary; follows MT.
Dan 9:15-17 (2 letters v. 15; 3 letters v. 16)	4QDanᵉ (4Q116)	DJD 16:289	Very fragmentary; follows MT.
Dan 10:5-13 (v. 10 N/R)	4QDanᶜ (4Q114)	Ulrich, *BASOR* 274: 3-26	Mostly follows MT.
Dan 10:8-16	6QDan (6Q7)	DJD 3:114-115	Fragmentary; mostly follows MT.
Dan 10:13-16	4QDanᶜ (4Q114)	Ulrich, *BASOR* 274: 3-26	Extremely fragmentary; follows MT.
Dan 10:16-20	4QDanª (4Q112)	Ulrich, *BASOR* 268: 17-37	Fragmentary; mostly follows MT.
Dan 10:21-11:2	4QDanᶜ (4Q114)	Ulrich, *BASOR* 274: 3-26	Mostly follows MT.
Dan 11:13-16	4QDanª (4Q112)	Ulrich, *BASOR* 268: 17-37	Very fragmentary; mostly follows MT.

Reference	*Scroll*	*Location*	*Comments*
Dan 11:13-17	4QDan^c (4Q114)	Ulrich, *BASOR* 274: 3-26	Very fragmentary; most listed readings are conjectures.
Dan 11:25-29	4QDan^c (4Q114)	Ulrich, *BASOR* 274: 3-26	Very fragmentary; follows MT.
Dan 11:32	4QFlor (4Q174)	DJD 5:54	יודעי אלוה יחזיקו A line added between two others. Identification may be questionable. MT reads אלהיו .
Dan 11:33-36, 38	6QDan (6Q7)	DJD 3:115	Very fragmentary; follows MT.
Dan 12:10	4QFlor (4Q174)	DJD 5:54	להרשי[ע] Only identification of Daniel is the pesher introduction to this word, ר כתוב בספר[דניאל הנביא . MT reads והרשיעו .
Hos 1:6-2:5 (3 letters 1:8)	4QXII^d (4Q79)	DJD 15:255	Fragmentary; all non-MT readings are unique, many spelling errors.
Hos 1:7-2:5	4QXII^d (4Q79)	Photo: Wolff, *Hosea* v; text: Sinclair, *BASOR* 239:61-65	Fragmentary; generally follows MT.
Hos 2:1-5 (v. 3 N/R)	4QXII^g (4Q82)	DJD 15:276	Fragmentary; mostly follows MT.
Hos 2:8 (?)	8HevXII gr (8Hev1), fragment 1	Lifshitz, *IEJ* 12:202-206	αvο ευρη

Reference	Scroll	Location	Comments
Hos 2:8-9	4QpHos^a (4Q166)	DJD 5:31	בסירים ונתיבותיה ישוך כיא Omits את גדרה in v. 8.
Hos 2:10-14	4QpHos^a (4Q166)	DJD 5:31-32	Follows MT except omits לה in v. 10b, and reads מלכסות in v. 11 (=LXX).
Hos 2:13-15 (1 letter v. 13)	4QXII^c (4Q78)	DJD 15:239	Very fragmentary; identical to MT.
Hos 2:14-19	4QXII^g (4Q82)	DJD 15:277	Very fragmentary; may read א[י]ת for חית v. 14 (spelling?); otherwise follows MT.
Hos 2:22-4:1 (2 letters 3:2)	4QXII^g (4Q82)	DJD 15:277-278	Very fragmentary; follows MT.
Hos 3:2-4	4QXII^c (4Q78)	DJD 15:240	ים ולתך ים רבים יש
Hos 4:1-5:1 (4 letters 4:1; 1 letter 4:2; 4:5,8 N/R; 2 letters 4:10; 4 letters 4:11; 1 letter 4:12; 4 letters 4:13; 4:14,17 N/R; 4 letters 4:18; 3 letters 4:19)	4QXII^c (4Q78)	DJD 15:140	יוש[בי 4:3 (=LXX); otherwise mostly follows MT.
Hos 4:10-11	4QXII^g (4Q82)	DJD 15:279	הזנו ב
Hos 4:13-14	4QXII^g (4Q82)	DJD 15:279	Extremely fragmentary; follows MT.
Hos 5:13-15	4QpHos^b (4Q167)	DJD 5:33	Fragmentary; follows MT.

Reference	*Scroll*	*Location*	*Comments*
Hos 6:3-4 (1 letter v. 4)	4QXII^g (4Q82)	DJD 15:280	Extremely fragmentary; follows MT.
Hos 6:4	4QpHos^b (4Q167)	DJD 5:33	עשה לכה[מ]ה Follows MT.
Hos 6:7	4QpHos^b (4Q167)	DJD 5:34	ברו ברית Identical to MT.
Hos 6:8-7:1 (2 letters 6:8; 3 letters 6:11; 2 letters 7:1)	4QXII^g (4Q82)	DJD 15:280	Extremely fragmentary; follows MT.
Hos 6:9	4QpIsa^c (4Q163)	DJD 5:24	כיחכה איש גדוד[ים MT reads כחכי.
Hos 6:9-10	4QpHos^b (4Q167)	DJD 5:34	Mostly pesher; identical to MT.
Hos 7:13-8:1 (1 letter 8:1)	4QXII^g (4Q82)	DJD 15:281	Fragmentary; several unique readings.
Hos 7:12-13	4QXII^c (4Q78)	DJD 15:241	Of no textual value.
Hos 7:12-13	4QXII^g (4Q82)	DJD 15:280	שְׁמַע להם
Hos 8:6-7	4QpHos^b (4Q167)	DJD 5:34	Fragmentary; follows MT.
Hos 8:13-14	4QpHos^b (4Q167)	DJD 5:34-35	בו וישכ Of no textual value.
Hos 9:1-4	4QXII^g (4Q82)	DJD 15:281	ת דגן גר יהוה וש ל[ ]ה
Hos 9:9-17	4QXII^g (4Q82)	DJD 15:282	Fragmentary; follows MT.
Hos 10:1-14 (v. 7 N/R; 1 letter v. 14)	4QXII^g (4Q82)	DJD 15:282	Fragmentary; mostly follows MT.

Reference	Scroll	Location	Comments
Hos 11:2-5 (1 letter v. 2; 4 letters v. 3; 3 letters v. 5)	4QXII^g (4Q82)	DJD 15:283	Very fragmentary; follows MT.
Hos 11:6-11 (2 letters v. 6; v. 7 N/R)	4QXII^g (4Q82)	DJD 15:286	Very fragmentary; several unique readings.
Hos 12:1-13:1 (4 letters 12:2; 4 letters 12:5; 12:6 N/R; 12:11 N/R; 3 letters 12:14, 15; 3 letters 13:1)	4QXII^g (4Q82)	DJD 15:286	Very fragmentary; mostly follows MT.
Hos 13:3-10 (2 letters v. 3; v. 6 N/R; v. 9 N/R; 3 letters v. 10)	4QXII^c (4Q78)	DJD 15:241	Includes LXX addition v. 4, though there is some discrepancy between DJD's report of the addition and *BHS*'s note: DJD addition includes ו[אנוכי העלותיכה but *BHS* erroneously does not report this part; otherwise follows MT.
Hos 13:6-8 (?)	4QXII^g (4Q82)	DJD 15:287	Of no textual value.
Hos 13:11-13	4QXII^g (4Q82)	DJD 15:288	Of no textual value.
Hos 13:15b-14:1a, 3-6	4QXII^c (4Q78)	Testuz, *Semitica* 5:37-38	Follows MT.
Hos 13:15-14:6 (14:2, 5 N/R)	4QXII^c (4Q78)	DJD 15:242	Very fragmentary; mostly follows MT.
Hos 14:9-10 (3 letters v. 9)	4QXII^g (4Q82)	DJD 15:288	Very fragmentary; follows MT.

Reference	Scroll	Location	Comments
Joel 1:10-2:1	4QXII^c (4Q78)	DJD 15:242-243	Very fragmentary; פורות 1:17 (=LXX); other readings are all unique.
Joel 1:12-14	4QXII^g (4Q82)	DJD 15:288	Fragmentary; follows MT.
Joel 1:14 (?)	8ḤevXII gr (8Ḥev1), fragment 3	Lifshitz, *IEJ* 12:202-206	ους πα ς οικου θ
Joel 2:2-13 (v. 4 N/R)	4QXII^g (4Q82)	DJD 15:289	Fragmentary; mostly follows MT.
Joel 2:8-10	4QXII^c (4Q78)	DJD 15:243	Very fragmentary; identical to MT.
Joel 2:10-23 (v. 15 N/R; 1 letter v. 21; 1 letter v. 23)	4QXII^c (4Q78)	DJD 15:244	Very fragmentary; adds ואכלתמה above the line v. 19; other non-MT readings are unique.
Joel 2:13	4Q266	DJD 18:76	Follows MT.
Joel 2:13	4Q270	DJD 18:163	Follows MT.
Joel 2.20	Mur XII (Mur 88)	DJD 2:184	Fragmentary; identical to MT.
Joel 2:26-4:16	Mur XII (Mur 88)	DJD 2:184-185	Nearly complete; follows MT except ועל for MT ואל in 4:3 (=LXX).
Joel 4:4-9 (v. 6 N/R)	4QXII^g (4Q82)	DJD 15:292	Very fragmentary; mostly follows MT.
Joel 4:6-20 (v. 7 N/R; v. 8 N/R?; v. 11 N/R; v. 20 N/R)	4QXII^c (4Q78)	DJD 15:245	Very fragmentary; vv. 6b-8 omitted?; v. 11 erased?; numerous unique readings.
Joel 4:11-14	4QXII^g (4Q82)	DJD 15:292	No more than 5 letters per verse; of no textual value.
Joel 4:17	4QXII^g (4Q82)	DJD 15:292	עֵת

Reference	*Scroll*	*Location*	*Comments*
Joel 4:19-20	4QXII^g (4Q82)	DJD 15:293	מחמס בני י תשב

Amos 1:2-3	5QAmos (5Q4)	DJD 3:173	Fragmentary; follows MT.
Amos 1:3-5	5QAmos (5Q4)	DJD 3:173	Fragmentary; mostly follows MT.
Amos 1:3-7	4QXII^g (4Q82)	DJD 15:294	Very fragmentary; follows MT.
Amos 1:5 (?)	8ḤevXII gr (8Ḥev1) fragment 2	Lifshitz, *IEJ* 12:202-206	ρε ακοψ τευθη
Amos 1:5-21	Mur XII (Mur 88)	DJD 2:185-186	Fragmentary; follows MT.
Amos 1:9-2:1 (3 letters 1:9; 4 letters 1:15; 1 letter 2:1)	4QXII^g (4Q82)	DJD 15:294-295	Very fragmentary; mostly follows MT.
Amos 2:11-3:7 (4 letters 2:11; 3 letters 2:12; 3:3 N/R)	4QXII^c (4Q78)	DJD 15:246	Fragmentary; non-MT readings are unique.
Amos 3:8-4:2 (2 letters 3:14)	4QXII^c (4Q78)	DJD 15:247	Fragmentary; הביאן 4:1 (=LXX); other non-MT readings are unique.
Amos 6:13-14	4QXII^c (4Q78)	DJD 15:248	ד ב] [הְאָ נואם יהוה
Amos 7:1-4 (v. 3 N/R)	4QXII^c (4Q78)	DJD 15:248	Fragmentary; follows MT.
Amos 7:3-8:7	Mur XII (Mur 88)	DJD 2:186-187	Fragmentary; follows MT.

Reference	*Scroll*	*Location*	*Comments*
Amos 7:7-9	4QXII^c (4Q78)	DJD 15:248	Extremely fragmentary; appears to read שמתי v. 8 (=LXX).
Amos 7:12-16	4QXII^c (4Q78)	DJD 15:248	Very fragmentary; follows MT.
Amos 8:11-9:1	4QXII^g (4Q82)	DJD 15:307	Very fragmentary; follows MT.
Amos 8:11-9:15	Mur XII (Mur 88)	DJD 2:187-188	Follows MT.
Amos 9:5-6 (3 letters v. 5)	4QXII^g (4Q82)	DJD 15:307	Very fragmentary; follows MT with *Qere*; note that DJD does not mention the fragment of v. 5.
Amos 9:11	4QFlor (4Q174)	DJD 5:53	Only four words; follows MT.
Amos 9:14-15	4QXII^g (4Q82)	DJD 15:308	Fragmentary; follows MT.
Obad 1-21 (entire book)	Mur XII (Mur 88)	DJD 2:189	Nearly complete; only two certain variants from MT; v. 11 supports *Kethib* שערו over *Qere* שעריו.
Obad 1-5 (1 letter v. 5)	4QXII^g (4Q82)	DJD 15:308	Fragmentary; follows MT except תשים v. 5 (=LXX).
Obad 8-12 (2 letters v. 8; 3 letters v. 11; 1 letter v. 12)	4QXII^g (4Q82)	DJD 15:308	Extremely fragmentary; follows MT.
Obad 14-15	4QXII^g (4Q82)	DJD 15:308	Fragmentary; follows MT except שובו v. 15 (unique).

Reference	*Scroll*	*Location*	*Comments*
Jon 1:1-5 (4 letters v. 1)	4QXII^a (4Q76)	DJD 15:229	Very fragmentary; follows MT.
Jon 1:1-9 (3 letters v. 9)	4QXII^g (4Q82)	DJD 15:309-310	Fragmentary; follows MT except וְמָה v. 8 (=LXX).
Jon 1:1-3:2	Mur XII (Mur 88)	DJD 2:190-191	Good, near-complete text; follows MT with notable accuracy.
Jon 1:6-8	4QXII^f (4Q81)	DJD 15:268-269	Very fragmentary; follows MT.
Jon 1:7-8	4QXII^a (4Q76)	DJD 15:229	Very fragmentary; mostly follows MT.
Jon 1:9-10	4QXII^a (4Q76)	DJD 15:230	Very fragmentary; mostly follows MT.
Jon 1:10-16 (3 letters v. 15; 4 letters v. 16)	4QXII^f (4Q81)	DJD 15:269	Very fragmentary; follows MT.
Jon 1:14, 16	8HevXII gr (8Hev1)	Barthélemy, VTSup 10:170	]μα αθω[ον]φ[ο]βη[θη]σαν[και εθυσιασαν θ[υ]σιαν Strikingly follows MT. See Introduction.
Jon 1:15-2:1 (3 uncertain letters 1:15)	4QXII^a (4Q76)	DJD 15:230-231	Very fragmentary; follows MT.
Jon 2:1, 4-7	8HevXII gr (8Hev1)	Barthélemy, VTSup 10:170	Supports MT.
Jon 2:3-3:3 (4 letters 3:3)	4QXII^g (4Q82)	DJD 15:310-311	Fragmentary; numerous spelling oddities; adds נפשי after חיי 2:7 (unique).
Jon 2:7	4QXII^a (4Q76)	DJD 15:231	Fragmentary; identical to MT.

Reference	Scroll	Location	Comments
Jon 3:2	4QXII^a (4Q76)	DJD 15:231	אה כזות אשר אנכי ד Position of כזות (= זאת of LXX) is unique.
Jon 3:2-5	8HevXII gr (8Hev1) fragment 4	Lifshitz, *IEJ* 12:202-206	Fragmentary; follows MT.
Jon 3:2-4:11	Mur XII (Mur 88)	DJD 2:191-192	Nearly complete; follows MT.
Jon 3:7-10	8HevXII gr (8Hev1)	Barthélemy, VTSup 10:171	Supports MT.
Jon 4:1-2, 5	8HevXII gr (8Hev1)	Barthélemy, VTSup 10:171	Supports MT; reads יהוה for τὸν עσιοκύριον in v. 2.
Jon 4:5-11	4QXII^g (4Q82)	DJD 15:312	Very fragmentary; several unique readings; כעלות v. 7 (=Targum^mss).

Mic 1:1-5	1QpMic (1Q14)	DJD 1:77	Fragmentary; most cited readings based on proposed reconstructions. What is extant follows MT.
Mic 1:1-8	8HevXII gr (8Hev1)	Barthélemy, VTSup 10:171	Striking adherence to MT over LXX (see Introduction).
Mic 1:5-7	1QpMic (1Q14)	DJD 1:78	Fragmentary; follows MT.
Mic 1:5-3:4	Mur XII (Mur 88)	DJD 2:191-193	Follows MT except הלך for הולך in 2:7, and לא for לו in 2:11.
Mic 1:7	4QXII^g (4Q82)	DJD 15:313	וכל פסיל זונה
Mic 1:8-9	1QpMic (1Q14)	DJD 1:78	Fragmentary; follows MT.

Reference	*Scroll*	*Location*	*Comments*
Mic 1:12-15	4QXII^g (4Q82)	DJD 15:313	Extremely fragmentary; ללכ]יש v. 13 (unique); otherwise follows MT.
Mic 2:3-4	4QXII^g (4Q82)	DJD 15:313	Extremely fragmentary; follows MT with a couple of apparent scribal errors.
Mic 2:7-8	8HevXII gr (8Hev1)	Barthélemy, VTSup 10:172	Follows MT.
Mic 3:4-4:12	Mur XII (Mur 88)	DJD 2:193-194	Text very broken; follows MT.
Mic 3:5-6	8HevXII gr (8Hev1)	Barthélemy, VTSup 10:172	Follows MT.
Mic 3:12-4:2 (1 letter 4:2)	4QXII^g (4Q82)	DJD 15:314	Extremely fragmentary; follows MT.
Mic 4:3-5	8HevXII gr (8Hev1)	Barthélemy, VTSup 10:172	Follows MT.
Mic 4:6-10	8HevXII gr (8Hev1)	Barthélemy, VTSup 10:172	Strikingly literal translation of MT.
Mic 4:8-12	4QpMic (4Q168)	DJD 5:35	Very fragmentary; identical to MT.
Mic 4:12-6:7	Mur XII (Mur 88)	DJD 2:194-195	Fragmentary; follows MT except כאריה for באריה in 5:7.
Mic 4:13 (?)	1QpMic (1Q14)	DJD 1:79	May include pesher if identification is correct.
Mic 5:1-4	8HevXII gr (8Hev1)	Barthélemy, VTSup 10:172-173	Follows MT (see Introduction).
Mic 5:4-6	8HevXII gr (8Hev1)	Barthélemy, VTSup 10:173	Follows MT.
Mic 5:6-7	4QXII^g (4Q82)	DJD 15:314	Very fragmentary; follows MT.

Reference	Scroll	Location	Comments
Mic 6:11-7:17	Mur XII (Mur 88)	DJD 2:195-196	Text broken and fragmentary; generally follows MT.
Mic 6:14-16	1QpMic (1Q14)	DJD 1:79	Fragmentary; follows MT.
Mic 7:2	4Q271	DJD 18:178	רעהו for MT אחיהו; otherwise follows MT.
Mic 7:2-3	4QXII^g (4Q82)	DJD 15:315	Very fragmentary; follows MT.
Mic 7:6, 8-9, 17 (?)	1QpMic (1Q14)	DJD 1:79-80	Fragmentary; all identifications uncertain.
Mic 7:20	4QXII^g (4Q82)	DJD 125:315	3 letters; of no textual value.

Reference	Scroll	Location	Comments
Nah 1:1-2:12	Mur XII (Mur 88)	DJD 2:196-198	Mostly follows MT with one LXX reading (adds an article).
Nah 1.2	4Q270	DJD 18:158	הוא for MT יהוה; otherwise follows MT.
Nah 1:3-6	4QpNah (4Q169)	DJD 5:37	Fragmentary; follows MT.
Nah 1:7-9 (3 letters v. 9)	4QXII^g (4Q82)	DJD 15:315	Very fragmentary; follows MT.
Nah 1:9 (?)	8HevXII gr (8Hev1), fragment 5	Lifshitz, *IEJ* 12:202-206	ιζε σετ ι
Nah 2:5-14 (vv. 11-12 N/R)	8HevXII gr (8Hev1)	Barthélemy, VTSup 10:173	Strikingly supports MT over LXX. Note especially πυλαι των ποταμων in v. 7. LXX reads των πολεων; MT reads הנהרות.

Reference	*Scroll*	*Location*	*Comments*
Nah 2:8-9 (?)	8HevXII gr (8Hev1) fragment 6	Lifshitz, *IEJ* 12:202-206	ω και ν
Nah 2:9-11	4QXII^g (4Q82)	DJD 15:316	Very fragmentary; מימיה v. 9 (=LXX).
Nah 2:12-14	4QpNah (4Q169)	DJD 5:38	Fairly complete; much pesher; numerous spelling errors and nonsense readings.
Nah 2:13-3:19	Mur XII (Mur 88)	DJD 2:198	Generally follows MT.
Nah 3:1-3	4QXII^g (4Q82)	DJD 15:316	Averages 3 letters per verse; of no textual value.
Nah 3:1-5	4QpNah (4Q169)	DJD 5:38	Nearly complete; follows MT.
Nah 3:6-9	4QpNah (4Q169)	DJD 5:38-39	Generally follows MT.
Nah 3:6-17	8HevXII gr (8Hev1)	Barthélemy, VTSup 10:173-174	Follows MT.
Nah 3:10-12	4QpNah (4Q169)	DJD 5:39	Somewhat fragmentary; follows MT with numerous spelling errors.
Nah 3:14	4QpNah (4Q169)	DJD 5:42	One line; only three certain letters; of no textual value.
Nah 3:17	4QXII^g (4Q82)	DJD 15:316	Very fragmentary; follows MT.

Hab 1:2-17	1QpHab	Cross, *Scrolls from Qumran Cave 1*; see also Brownlee, *Text of Habakkuk*	Mostly follows MT.

Reference	Scroll	Location	Comments
Hab 1:3-2:11	Mur XII (Mur 88)	DJD 2:199	Very fragmentary; follows MT.
Hab 1:5-11	8HevXII gr (8Hev1)	Barthélemy, VTSup 10:174	Strikingly favors MT over LXX.
Hab 1:14-17	8HevXII gr (8Hev1)	Barthélemy, VTSup 10:174-175	Follows MT.
Hab 2:1-8	8HevXII gr (8Hev1)	Barthélemy, VTSup 10:175	Literal translation of MT.
Hab 2:1-20	1QpHab	Cross, *Scrolls from Qumran Cave 1*; see also Brownlee, *Text of Habakkuk*	Mostly follows MT.
Hab 2:4?	4QXII^g (4Q82)	DJD 15:316	יִשְׁרָה נפשׁ
Hab 2:13-20	8HevXII gr (8Hev1)	Barthélemy, VTSup 10:175-176	Follows MT.
Hab 2:18-3.19	Mur XII (Mur 88)	DJD 2:200	Follows MT; curious reading זרמו מים עבות in 3·10 (cf. Ps 77:18).
Hab 3:9-15 (vv. 11,12 N/R)	8HevXII gr (8Hev1)	Barthélemy, VTSup 10:176	Literal translation of MT.

Zeph 1:1	Mur XII (Mur 88)	DJD 2:200	דְּבָן]הָוָה אֲשֶׁר הָיָה וֹ בֶּן אֲ Identical to MT.
Zeph 1:1-2	4QXII^b (4Q77)	DJD 15:234	כלך יהודה אסף
Zeph 1:1-5	8HevXII gr (8Hev1)	Barthélemy, VTSup 10:176	Literal translation of MT.

Reference	Scroll	Location	Comments
Zeph 1:11-3:6	Mur XII (Mur 88)	DJD 2:200-201	Fragmentary; generally follows MT.
Zeph 1:12-13	4QpZeph (4Q170)	DJD 5:42	One broken line; follows MT.
Zeph 1:13-17	8HevXII gr (8Hev1)	Barthélemy, VTSup 10:177	Strikingly literal translation of MT.
Zeph 1:18-2:2	1QpZeph (1Q15)	DJD 1:80	Fragmentary; follows MT.
Zeph 2:9-10	8HevXII gr (8Hev1)	Barthélemy, VTSup 10:177	Consistently supports MT.
Zeph 2:13-15	4QXII^b (4Q77)	DJD 15:234	Very fragmentary; follows MT except ויאב for ויאבד v. 13 (scribal error).
Zeph 2:15-3:2 (3:1 N/R)	4QXII^c (4Q78)	DJD 15:249	Very fragmentary; follows MT.
Zeph 3:3-5	4QXII^g (4Q82)	DJD 15:317	Of no textual value.
Zeph 3:6-7	8HevXII gr (8Hev1)	Barthélemy, VTSup 10:177	Follows MT.
Zeph 3:8-20	Mur XII (Mur 88)	DJD 2:202	Fairly complete; follows MT except על העמים for אל עמים in v. 9.
Zeph 3:9	4Q464	DJD 19:218	Very fragmentary; follows MT.
Zeph 3:19-20	4QXII^b (4Q77)	DJD 15:235	Fragmentary; identical to MT.

Hag 1:1-2	4QXII^b (4Q77)	DJD 15:235	Fragmentary; follows MT except spelling variation לדריוש for לדריהש.

Reference	Scroll	Location	Comments
Hag 1:1-11	Mur XII (Mur 88)	DJD 2:202-203	Follows MT.
Hag 1:12-2:10	Mur XII (Mur 88)	DJD 2:203-204	Fragmentary; follows MT.
Hag 2:2-4 (4 letters v. 4)	4QXII^b (4Q77)	DJD 15:236	Very fragmentary; identical to MT.
Hag 2:12-23	Mur XII (Mur 88)	DJD 2:204-205	Follows MT.
Hag 2:18-19	4QXII^e (4Q80)	DJD 15:259	יום גורה נשא
Hag 2:20-21	4QXII^e (4Q80)	DJD 15:259	בעש פחת י

Reference	Scroll	Location	Comments
Zech 1:1-4	Mur XII (Mur 88)	DJD 2:205	Fragmentary; identical to MT.
Zech 1:1-4 (v. 2 N/R)	8HevXII gr (8Hev1)	Barthélemy, VTSup 10:177	Consistently supports MT over LXX.
Zech 1:4-6	4QXII^e (4Q80)	DJD 15:260	Very fragmentary; omits לנו v. 6.
Zech 1:9-10	4QXII^e (4Q80)	DJD 15:260	Of no textual value.
Zech 1:13-14	8HevXII gr (8Hev1)	Barthélemy, VTSup 10:177	αγα προσ[ ]γελ Of no textual value.
Zech 1:13-14	4QXII^e (4Q80)	DJD 15:261	Of no textual value.
Zech 2:2,7	8HevXII gr (8Hev1)	Barthélemy, VTSup 10:177	No full words remain; supports MT over LXX.
Zech 2:10-14	4QXII^e (4Q80)	DJD 15:261	Very fragmentary; follows MT.

Reference	*Scroll*	*Location*	*Comments*
Zech 2:16-3:7 (3:2, 3 N/R)	8HevXII gr (8Hev1)	Barthélemy, VTSup 10:178	Supports MT over LXX.
Zech 3:1-2 (?)	8HevXII gr (8Hev1), fragment 7	Lifshitz, *IEJ* 12:202-206	αυ αιειπεν πιτι
Zech 3:2-4:4 (2 letters 3:3; 3 letters 3:5,6)	4QXII^e (4Q80)	DJD 15:262	Very fragmentary; mostly follows MT.
Zech 4:8-9 (?)	8HevXII gr (8Hev1), fragment 8	Lifshitz, *IEJ* 12:202-206	ς και ζ ọ/ọ̣ [?] και θ/η [?] Lifshitz reads O in line 2, but what remains looks more like C. In line 4, Lifshitz reads Θ, but lack of curvature on the vertical strokes suggests that it is actually H.
Zech 5:8-6:5 (3 letters 5:8; 1 letter 6:1; 3 letters 6:2)	4QXII^e (4Q80)	DJD 15:263	Very fragmentary; an odd assortment of readings.
Zech 8:2-4	4QXII^e (4Q80)	DJD 15:264	Very fragmentary; follows MT.
Zech 8:6-7	4QXII^e (4Q80)	DJD 15:264	Extremely fragmentary; הרנם v. 6 (=LXX).
Zech 8:19-23 (v. 22 N/R)	8HevXII gr (8Hev1)	Barthélemy, VTSup 10:178	Consistently supports MT.
Zech 8:21 (?)	8HevXII gr (8Hev1), fragment 9	Lifshitz, *IEJ* 12:202-206	ατοικ ελεγ τησα
Zech 8:24-9:4	8HevXII gr (8Hev1)	Barthélemy, VTSup 10:178	Favors MT over LXX.

Reference	Scroll	Location	Comments
Zech 10:11-12:2	4QXII^g (4Q82)	DJD 15:317	Extremely fragmentary; follows MT except יתהל[לו 10:12 (=MT^mss, LXX); note bracketing typo in DJD transcription of line 1, see plate instead.
Zech 11:11	4QpIsa^c (4Q163)	DJD 5:23	Fragmentary; follows MT.
Zech 12:1-3 (1 letter v. 3)	4QXII^g (4Q82)	DJD 15:317	Extremely fragmentary; follows MT.
Zech 12:7-12 (1 letter v. 7)	4QXII^e (4Q80)	DJD 15:264	Very fragmentary; adds ירושלים על יהודה in the margin (?); otherwise follows MT.
Zech 13:9	4QTanhumim (4Q176)	DJD 5:64	Fragmentary; follows MT.
Zech 14:18	4QXII^a (4Q76)	DJD 15:223	Very fragmentary; identical to MT.

Reference	Scroll	Location	Comments
Mal 1:10	4Q266	DJD 18:41	Very fragmentary; what remains follows MT (but see DJD reconstruction based on CD).
Mal 1:13-14	5QapMal (5Q10)	DJD 3:180	Mostly pesher; of no textual value.
Mal 2:10	4Q265	DJD 35:63	Very fragmentary; identical to MT.
Mal 2:10-14	4QXII^a (4Q76)	DJD 15:223	Very fragmentary; עד for ער v. 11 (=LXX); מאון for מאין v. 13 (LXX? Or letter confusion?); several unique readings including omission of אשר...בה v. 14.

Reference	Scroll	Location	Comments
Mal 2:10-16	4QXII^a (4Q76)	Fuller, *JBL* 110: 47-57	Favors LXX with some unique readings.
Mal 2:15-3:4	4QXII^a (4Q76)	DJD 15:224-225	Very poorly written; numerous unique readings, only one sure LXX reading.
Mal 3:6-7(?) (3 letters v. 6)	4QXII^c (4Q78)	DJD 15:251	Very fragmentary; textual value questionable.
Mal 3:5-14	4QXII^a (4Q76)	DJD 15:226-227	Fragmentary; non-MT readings are unique.
Mal 3:14-24 (3 letters v. 14; 2 letters v. 18)	4QXII^a (4Q76)	DJD 15:228	Very fragmentary; many unique readings.
Mal 3:16-18	4QCommentary on Malachi (4Q253a)	DJD 22:214	Very fragmentary; appears to generally follow MT.

SELECTED BIBLIOGRAPHY

Alexander, Philip S. and Geza Vermes. *Qumran Cave 4: XIX, Serekh Ha-Yaḥad and Two Related Texts*. Discoveries in the Judaean Desert 26. Oxford: Clarendon, 1998.

Allegro, John M. *Qumran Cave 4: I (4Q158—4Q186)*. Discoveries in the Judaean Desert 5. Oxford: Clarendon, 1968.

Attridge, H. *et al. Qumran Cave 4. VIII: Parabiblical Texts, Part 1*. Discoveries in the Judaean Desert 13. Oxford: Clarendon, 1994.

Baillet, Maurice. *Qumrân Grotte 4. III (4Q482—4Q520)*. Discoveries in the Judaean Desert 7. Oxford: Clarendon, 1982.

Baillet, M., J. T. Milik, and R. de Vaux. *Les 'Petites Grottes' de Qumrân: Exploration de la falaise, Les grottes 2Q, 3Q, 5Q, 6Q, 7Q a 10Q, Le rolueau de cuivre*. Discoveries in the Judaean Desert 3. 2 vols. Oxford: Clarendon, 1962.

Barthélemy, Dominique. *Les Devanciers d'Aquila: Première publication intégrale du texte des fragments du Dodécapropheton*. Vetus Testamentum Supplements 10. Leiden: E. J. Brill, 1963.

Barthélemy, D. and J. T. Milik. *Qumran Cave 1*. Discoveries in the Judaean Desert 1. Oxford: Clarendon, 1955.

Baumgarten, Joseph M. *Qumran Cave 4. XIII: The Damascus Document*. Discoveries in the Judaean Desert 18. Oxford: Clarendon, 1996.

Baumgarten, Joseph M. *et al.*, eds. *Qumran Cave 4. XXV: Halakhic Texts*. Discoveries in the Judaean Desert 35. Oxford: Clarendon, 1999.

Benoit, P., J. T. Milik, and R. de Vaux. *Les Grottes de Murabba'ât*. Discoveries in the Judaean Desert 2. 2 vols. Oxford: Clarendon, 1961.

Broshi, Magen *et al. Qumran Cave 4. XIV: Parabiblical Texts Part 2*. Discoveries in the Judaean Desert 19. Oxford: Clarendon, 1995.

Brownlee, William H. *The Text of Habakkuk in the Ancient Commentary from Qumran*. Journal of Biblical Literature Monograph Series 11. Philadelphia: Society of Biblical Literature, 1959

———. "The Scroll of Ezekiel from the Eleventh Qumran Cave." *Revue de Qumran* 4 (1963):11-28.

Burchard, Christoph. "Gen 35 und 36 MT aus der Wüste Juda (Naḥal Ḥever, Cave of the Letters?)." *Zeitschrift für die alttestamentliche Wissenschaft* 78 (1966):71-75.

Burrows, Millar. *The Dead Sea Scrolls of St. Mark's Monastery*. 2 vols. New Haven: American Schools of Oriental Research, 1950-1951.

157

Chazon, Esther, *et al. Qumran Cave 4. XX: Poetical and Liturgical Texts, Part 2.* Discoveries in the Judaean Desert 29. Oxford: Clarendon, 1999.

Cotton, Hannah M. and Ada Yardeni. *Aramaic, Hebrew and Greek Documentary Texts from Naḥal Ḥever and Other Sites.* Discoveries in the Judaean Desert 27. Oxford: Clarendon, 1997. [Not cited in the catalog]

Cross, Frank Moore. "A New Qumran Biblical Fragment Related to the Original Hebrew Underlying the Septuagint." *Bulletin of the American Schools of Oriental Research* 132 (December 1953):15-26.

―――. "The Oldest Manuscripts from Qumran." *Journal of Biblical Literature* 74 (1955):147-172. Reprinted in *Qumran and the History of the Biblical Text*, eds. Frank Moore Cross and Shemaryahu Talmon, 147-176. Cambridge, MA: Harvard University, 1975.

―――. *The Ancient Library of Qumran and Modern Biblical Studies.* Rev. ed. Garden City, NY: Doubleday, 1961. Reprint; Grand Rapids, MI: Baker Book House, 1980.

―――. *Scrolls from the Wilderness of the Dead Sea.* Smithsonian Exhibit Catalogue. Berkeley, CA: University of California for the American Schools of Oriental Research, 1965.

Cross, F. M., *et al.*, ed. *Scrolls from Qumran Cave I: The Great Isaiah Scroll, the Order of the Community, the Pesher to Habakkuk.* Jerusalem: Albright Institute of Archaeological Research, 1972.

Elgvin, Torleif, *et al.*, ed. *Qumran Cave 4. XV: Sapiential Texts, Part 1.* Discoveries in the Judaean Desert 20. Oxford: Clarendon, 1997.

Eshel, Esther, *et al.*, ed. *Qumran Cave 4. VI: Poetical and Liturgical Texts, Part 1.* Discoveries in the Judaean Desert 11. Oxford: Clarendon, 1998.

Fitzmyer, Joseph A. *The Genesis Apocryphon of Qumran Cave 1: A Commentary.* Rome: Pontifical Biblical Institute, 1966.

―――. *The Dead Sea Scrolls: Major Publications and Tools for Study.* Rev. ed. Society of Biblical Literature Resources for Biblical Study 20. Atlanta: Scholars Press, 1990.

Freedman, David Noel. "Variant Readings in the Leviticus Scroll from Qumran Cave 11." *Catholic Biblical Quarterly* 36 (1974):525-534.

Freedman, D. N., and K. A. Mathews. *The Paleo-Hebrew Leviticus Scroll (11QpaleoLev).* Winona Lake: ASOR, 1985. [Cited in the Catalog as Freedman, *11QpaleoLev*]

Fuller, Russell. "Text-Critical Problems in Malachi 2:10-16." *Journal of Biblical Literature* 110 (1991):47-57.

García Martínez, Florentino, E. J. C. Tigchelaar, and A. S. van der Woude. *Manuscripts from Qumran Cave 11 (11Q2-18, 11Q20-30).* Discoveries in the Judaean Desert 23. Oxford: Clarendon, 1997.

García Martínez, Florentino, and E. J. C. Tigchelaar. *The Dead Sea Scrolls Study Edition.* 2 vols. Leiden: Brill, 1997-98.

Janzen, J. Gerald. *Studies in the Text of Jeremiah.* Cambridge: Harvard University, 1973.

Lifshitz, B. "The Greek Documents from the Cave of Horror." *Israel Exploration Journal* 12 (1962):201-207.

Milik, J. T. "Deux documents inédits du Désert de Juda." *Biblica* 38 (1957):245-268 and plates I-IV.

———. "Le travail d'édition des manuscrits du Désert de Juda." In *Volume du congres, Strasbourg 1956*, pp. 17-26. Vetus Testamentum Supplements 4. Leiden: E. J. Brill, 1957.

———. "Fragment d'une source du Psautier (4Q Ps 89) et fragments des Jubilés, du Document de Damas, d'un Phylactère dans la grotte 4 de Qumrân." *Revue biblique* 73 (1966):94-106 and plates I-III.

———. "II. Tefillin, Mezuzot et Targums (4Q128—4Q157)." In *Qumrân Grotte 4. II.* Discoveries in the Judaean Desert 6. Oxford: Clarendon, 1977.

Muilenburg, James. "Fragments of Another Qumran Isaiah Scroll." *Bulletin of the American Schools of Oriental Research* 135 (October 1954):28-32.

———. "A Qoheleth Scroll from Qumran." *Bulletin of the American Schools of Oriental Research* 135 (October 1954):20-28.

Ploeg, J. P. M. van der. "Le Psaume XCI dans une recension du Qumrân." *Revue biblique* 72 (1965):210-217 and plates VIII-IX.

———. "Fragments d'un manuscrit de Psaumes de Qumran (11QPs^b)." *Revue biblique* 74 (1967):408-412 and plate XVIII.

———. "Lév. IX,23-X,2 dans un texte de Qumran." In *Bibel und Qumran: Beiträge zur Erforschung der Beziehungen zwischen Bibel- und Qumranwissenschaft: Hans Bardtke zum 22. 9. 1966*, ed. S. Wagner, 153-155. Berlin: Evangelische Haupt-Bibelgesellschaft, 1968.

Ploeg, J. P. M. van der, and A. S. van der Woude. *Le Targum de Job de la Grotte XI de Qumran.* Leiden: E. J. Brill, 1971.

Puech, Emile. *Qumran Grotte 4. XVIII: Textes Hebreux.* Discoveries in the Judaean Desert 25. Oxford: Clarendon, 1998.

Qimron, E. and J. Strugnell. *Qumran Cave 4. V.* Discoveries in the Judaean Desert 10. Oxford: Clarendon, 1994.

Sanders, J. A. *The Psalms Scroll of Qumrân Cave 11 (11QPs^a).* Discoveries in the Judaean Desert 4. 2 vols. Oxford: Clarendon, 1965.

———. "Palestinian Manuscripts 1947-1967." *Journal of Biblical Literature* 86 (1967):431-440.

———. *The Dead Sea Psalms Scroll.* Ithaca: Cornell University, 1967.

Sinclair, Lawrence A. "A Qumran Biblical Fragment: Hosea 4QXII^d (Hosea 1:7-2:5)." *Bulletin of the American Schools of Oriental Research* 239 (Summer 1980):61-65.

Skehan, P. W. "A Fragment of the 'Song of Moses' (Deut. 32) from Qumran." *Bulletin of the American Schools of Oriental Research* 136 (December 1954):12-15.

———. "The Qumran Manuscripts and Textual Criticism." In *Volume du congres: Strasbourg 1956, pp. 148-160.* Vetus Testamentum Supplements 4. Leiden: E. J. Brill, 1957. Reprinted in *Qumran and the History of the Biblical Text*, eds. Frank Moore Cross and Shemaryahu Talmon, 212-225. Cambridge, MA: Harvard

————. "A Psalm Manuscript from Qumran (4QPsᵇ)." *Catholic Biblical Quarterly* 26 (1964):313-322.

————. "The Biblical Scrolls from Qumran and the Text of the Old Testament." *Biblical Archaeologist* 28 (1965):87-100. Reprinted in *Qumran and the History of the Biblical Text*, ed. Frank Moore Cross and Shemaryahu Talmon, 264-277. Cambridge, MA: Harvard University, 1975. Skehan, P. W., E. Ulrich, and J. E. Sanderson. *Qumran Cave 4. IV: Paleo-Hebrew and Greek Biblical Manuscripts.* Discoveries in the Judaean Desert 9. Oxford: Clarendon, 1992.

Skehan, P. W., E. Ulrich, and P. W. Flint. "Two Manuscripts of Psalm 119 from Qumran Cave 4," *Revue de Qumran* 64:16 (Dec 1995):477-486.

Starcky, J. "Psaumes apocryphes de la grotte 4 de Qumrân (4QPsᶠ vii-x)." *Revue biblique* 73 (1966):353-371 and plate XIII.

Strugnell, John, Daniel J. Harrington, and Torlief Elgvin. *Qumran Cave 4. XXIV: 4QInstruction (Musar leMevin): 4Q415ff.* Discoveries in the Judaean Desert 34. Oxford: Clarendon, 1999.

Sukenik, E. L. *The Dead Sea Scrolls of the Hebrew University.* Jerusalem: Magnes, 1955.

Testuz, Michel. "Deux fragments inédits des manuscrits de la Mer Morte." *Semitica* 5 (1955):37-38 with plate.

Talmon, Shemaryahu. "קטעי שתי מגילות של ספר ויקרא ממצדה." ["Portions of Two Scrolls of the Book of Leviticus from Masada."] *Eretz Israel* 24 (1993): 99-110.

Tov, Emanuel. *The Greek Minor Prophets Scroll from Naḥal Ḥever (8ḤevXII gr).* Discoveries in the Judaean Desert 8. Oxford: Clarendon, 1990.

Ulrich, Eugene Charles. *The Qumran text of Samuel and Josephus.* Missoula: Scholars Press, 1978.

————. "4QSamᶜ: A Fragmentary Manuscript of 2 Samuel 14-15 from the Scribe of the *Serek Hay-yaḥad* (1QS)." *Bulletin of the American Schools of Oriental Research* 235 (Summer 1979):1-25.

————. "Daniel Manuscripts from Qumran. Part 1: A Preliminary Edition of 4QDanᵃ." *Bulletin of the American Schools of Oriental Research* 268 (November 1987) 17-37.

————. "Daniel Manuscripts from Qumran. Part 2: Preliminary Editions of 4QDanᵇ and 4QDanᶜ." *Bulletin of the American Schools of Oriental Research* 274 (1989):3-26.

Ulrich, Eugene Charles and F. M. Cross. *Qumran Cave 4. VII: Genesis to Numbers.* Discoveries in the Judaean Desert 12. Oxford: Clarendon, 1994.

Ulrich, Eugene Charles et al. *Qumran Cave 4. IX: Deuteronomy to Kings.* Discoveries in the Judaean Desert 14. Oxford: Clarendon, 1995.

————. *Qumran Cave 4. X: The Prophets.* Discoveries in the Judaean Desert 15. Oxford: Clarendon, 1997.

————. *Qumran Cave 4. XI: Psalms to Chronicles.* Discoveries in the Judaean Desert 16. Oxford: Clarendon, 2000.

Wolff, Hans Walter. *Hosea: A Commentary on the Book of the Prophet Hosea*. Trans. by Gary Stansell. Hermeneia. Philadelphia: Fortress, 1974.

Woude, A. S. van der. "Melchisedek als himmlische Erlösergestalt in den neugefundenen eschatologischen Midraschim aus Qumran — Höhle XI." כה [Kaf-He (25)], *1940-1965. Oudtestamentische Studiën* 14 (1965):354-373 with plate.

Würthwein, Ernst. *The Text of the Old Testament*. Trans. by Erroll F. Rhodes. Rev. ed. Grand Rapids: Eerdmans, 1979.

Yadin, Yigael. "The Expedition to the Judaean Desert, 1960:   Expedition D." *Israel Exploration Journal* 11 (1961):36-52.

————. "The Expedition to the Judaean Desert, 1961:   Expedition D — The Cave of the Letters." *Israel Exploration Journal* 12 (1962):227-257.

————. "The Excavation of Masada—1963/64, Preliminary Report." *Israel Exploration Journal* 15 (1965):1-120.

————. *Masada: Herod's Fortress and the Zealots' Last Stand*. New York: Random House, 1966.

————. *The Temple Scroll*. 3 vols. Jerusalem: Israel Exploration Society, 1983. Text references are from volume 2 unless otherwise indicated.